NM
12/12/06

Praise for
Leadership Passages

"One of the surprising aspects of this book is that these passages are predictable. In a typical career, all leaders will go through these passages. What this book does is provide leaders and those who aspire to senior leadership roles with the tools and techniques to help them understand and navigate personal change to achieve success in both their personal and business lives."

—COREY SEITZ, GLOBAL HEAD OF TALENT MANAGEMENT, NOVARTIS INTERNATIONAL AG

"The passages described by Dotlich, Noel, and Walker can make or break leaders. *Leadership Passages* helps readers become aware of these passages, learn what each entails, and acquire the skills necessary to navigate them successfully."

—RON JONASH, THE MONITOR GROUP

"*Leadership Passages* provides the missing link in leadership development. The authors recognize that these are key transitions in a leader's life that can catalyze tremendous growth. Too often, however, these transitions are ignored by individuals and organizations. Dotlich, Noel, and Walker offer great insight and advice on how to turn these passages into dynamic development experiences."

—DEBORRAH HIMSEL, VICE PRESIDENT, ORGANIZATION EFFECTIVENESS, AVON PRODUCTS, INC., AND AUTHOR, *LEADERSHIP SOPRANOS STYLE*

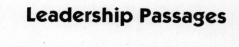

Leadership Passages

Leadership Passages

The Personal and Professional Transitions That Make or Break a Leader

David L. Dotlich

James L. Noel

Norman Walker

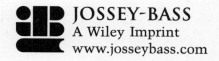

JOSSEY-BASS
A Wiley Imprint
www.josseybass.com

Published by Jossey-Bass
A Wiley Imprint
989 Market Street, San Francisco, CA 94103-1741   www.josseybass.com

Jossey-Bass books and products are available through most bookstores. To contact Jossey-Bass directly call our Customer Care Department within the U.S. at 800-956-7739, outside the U.S. at 317-572-3986 or fax 317-572-4002.

Jossey-Bass also publishes its books in a variety of electronic formats. Some content that appears in print may not be available in electronic books.

Library of Congress Cataloging-in-Publication Data
Dotlich, David L. (David Landreth), 1950-
  Leadership passages : the personal and professional transitions that make or break a leader / By David L. Dotlich, James L. Noel, Norman Walker.
    p. cm.
  Includes bibliographical references and index.
  ISBN 0-7879-7427-7 (alk. paper)
  1. Leadership. 2. Management. I. Noel, James L., 1943- II. Walker, Norman. III. Title.
  HD57.7.D675 2004
  658.4'092—dc22   2004012064

FIRST EDITION
HB Printing   10 9 8 7 65 4 3 2 1

Contents

Introduction

Adversity has the effect of eliciting talents which in prosperous circumstances would have lain dormant.

—Horace

One of us met recently with the new CEO of a large company who was profiling his team of direct reports. As the CEO talked with us, he focused on the skills and background of each direct report. Impressed with the diversity of the group, we asked, "Is there anything that everyone on your team has in common?"

He nodded. "At one point or another, each one of us has been fired."

The CEO said this proudly. To him, being fired was a badge of merit. His direct reports had been through tough times and learned from their experience. Because they had once been terminated, members of his team had grown personally and professionally. Difficult, unpredictable events had forced them to turn inward, address their flaws, and seek to understand how they may have contributed to their own dismissal. Termination had tested their resiliency— a trait crucial to leadership in competitive businesses. They were survivors.

We bring this up because, contrary to expectation, *successful careers are not continually successful*. In fact, even the most honored,

Note: We are indebted to the work of many people in considering how leaders actually develop, but several people deserve special mention. Morgan McCall was a pioneer in defining the importance of experience in developing leaders. Joseph Gabarro has researched and developed the concept of transition experiences in leadership effectiveness. Recently, our colleagues Dan Ciampa and Michael Watkins have also focused on transition experiences in leadership development.

effective, and acclaimed leaders go through periods of uncertainty, frustration, and failure. These periods can be triggered by both professional and personal events: coping with a bad boss, going through a divorce, taking over a demanding new assignment, living abroad, and many others. They can be periods of great growth and learning, or they can be times of stagnation, denial, and even regression. We call them *predictable, intense passages* because that is exactly what they are.

Thirteen Common Passages

We have selected thirteen passages to describe in this book; we've devoted a chapter to each one. But we don't intend the passages to represent a complete list of life and career experiences. Rather, we have chosen the thirteen that senior leaders mention most often and describe as particularly compelling or intense. If you work long enough, you will experience many of these passages, perhaps all of them. When you do, you will find them to be emotionally, intellectually, and even spiritually intense.

And they are *passages* because, as the word indicates, they take you from one place to another; you see the world and yourself differently after you've gone through the events and emotional states that define each passage. What you may *not* experience is permission to discuss these experiences openly and share your insights with others, because many companies today prefer to avoid addressing either the passages or their significance.

Our goal is to help you understand, learn from, and navigate the passages successfully. If you do, you will dramatically increase your leadership effectiveness. If you don't, you'll risk bypassing the most important leadership development experience you can face: your own life.

Our Sources of Insight

We've based our observations and advice on the experiences of real executives who have gone through these predictable, intense passages. We have interviewed over seventy-five managers about their own development as a leader and coached hundreds more in CDR International/Mercer Delta leadership programs that are conducted every week throughout the world for global companies such as Novartis, Merck, Dell, Johnson & Johnson, and many others. In these programs, we have the chance to work intensively with senior executives who have opened up to us about their lives and leadership experiences. These are real executives, and we have collected their stories through one-on-one interviews and ongoing conversation.

In these pages, we'll tell the stories they shared with us. In some instances, we'll disguise identities because of the personal nature of the stories and our agreement to maintain confidence. In other instances, executives have given us permission to use their names. This is an especially courageous act, because some of these individuals are revealing mistakes and failures, along with their deeply emotional reactions to them. Some of these leaders have been specifically interviewed for this book; others have been our clients and colleagues. We are especially grateful to those who agreed to be interviewed for this book: Bill George, former chairman and CEO of Medtronic; Joseph Beradino, former chairman and CEO of Arthur Andersen; Robert Glynn, chairman and CEO of Pacific Gas & Electric; Thomas Ebeling, CEO of Novartis Pharmaceuticals, and Ray Viault, vice chairman, General Mills.

Our Credentials

All three of us have been in senior positions with major companies, including Honeywell International, General Electric, Citicorp, Ford, Kraft, and Novartis. More recently, we've served as business advisers and executive development consultants, primarily with CDR International and Mercer Delta Consulting, to many major corporations, including Intel, Nike, and Bank of America. We've also been coaches to CEOs and other top executives within these organizations. In these personal, advisory relationships, we've been privileged to see well-known global leaders from a different perspective—often able to glimpse what is beneath the role and the public face. The content of these private conversations has both inspired and informed this book.

Some of the tales we'll tell are cautionary in nature. Although the passages may be predictable, an individual's response is not. There are dangers to a career of going through a passage in intellectually or emotionally dishonest ways. Denial may seem useful in the short term, but, in the long run, honestly acknowledging the extraordinary challenge of leadership passages is most beneficial. Many of the stories provide hope, as well as a roadmap for dealing with setbacks and perplexing, unfamiliar situations. By employing the techniques we have used to help leaders meet these challenges, you'll be in a better position to deal with whatever work and life may put in your way.

What to Expect from the Passages

If you've been an executive for any length of time, you've already gone through one or more passages. Whether it was a professional passage such as receiving a stretch assignment or a personal one such as finding a satisfying balance between work and family, you may already have a sense of the power and possibility of a passage. But it's possible that you went through passages unconsciously, without fully understanding what they entail. Or you may have been encouraged to "keep going" and, as a result, denied yourself the richness, significance, and growth inherent in significant life and leadership events, even when painful. If that is the case for you, it may be because we live and work in organizations that prize success above all else, defining leadership "development" in narrow, cognitive, and carefully prescribed terms. So although you may have shielded yourself from the pain and self-doubt that comes with the journey, you didn't get to reap the true leadership development benefits.

Our Approach to Leadership

Although many companies are now attempting to meet the challenge of defining and providing the right experiences for leaders, we prefer to take a broader view of how leaders are created. For individual leaders, being open to and aware of the learning that comes with each passage is critical. We know that this isn't always easy to do. As predictable as the passages are, their intensity in the moment they are lived is intimidating. Even the smartest, most effective leaders can react to adversity by citing unforeseen circumstances, other people, or just bad luck. Unable to accept their own role in creating negative circumstances, they avoid the tough challenge of self-reflection by directing their energy toward finding a scapegoat (see *Why CEOs Fail*, by David Dotlich and Peter Cairo).

As "bad" as a passage may sound, it is not the event itself that hurts a career but how you react to it. It is how you handle working for a bad boss, being fired, or being acquired that determines whether the impact is positive or negative and whether you become a stronger leader or remain the same. Similarly, passages such as obtaining your first leadership position provide great opportunities; however, some people learn and grow because of their approach to the opportunity, and others merely get a new job.

With this in mind, let's look at the three characteristics that are common to the passages we selected to present in this book:

1. *Predictable:* The passages we describe are inevitable. You'll go through some of them more than once. And even though they're predictable, they occur in a random fashion; many can take you by surprise. What is also predictable is that they will be a mix of personal and professional events, of adverse situations, and new or diverse experiences.

Some of you may be surprised to find personal issues discussed in a leadership book. We've found, however, that the loss of a loved one, a divorce, and other significant life events have a tremendous impact on leadership performance and work effectiveness. To pretend these events have no impact, as individuals and organizations are wont to do, inhibits leadership development.

2. *Intense:* All the passages are emotionally and cognitively severe. Experiences as diverse as living in another country or becoming responsible for a business will push you out of your comfort zone. To respond productively to the intensity, you need to grow, and growth means change. If you respond negatively, a passage can destroy your career or even your marriage. The good news, though, is that this intensity is a wonderful catalyst for growth. Even after a keenly unpleasant event like being fired, intensity can propel you to change your behaviors in ways that prepare you much better for your next leadership role.

3. *Passages:* The word itself expresses transition and change. A passage can change your perspective; it can cause you to view work or yourself differently; it can motivate you to acquire new skills or try alternative behaviors in order to be more effective.

How Learning Can Lead to Success

On the surface, it seems as if the passage is taking us in one of two directions: toward success or failure. We mishandle a major assignment and move toward failure; we receive our first leadership role and move toward success. In reality, it may seem as though we're going in one direction but we're actually going in the other. Mishandling an assignment can cause us to reflect, to seek advice about why our leadership approach caused us to make a blunder. The knowledge gained turns us into a better leader. Conversely, we take on our first leadership role and make it work; our simple win makes us think we know enough; our arrogance prevents us from asking questions, being open to new ideas, and growing even more within the new role.

Failing to Learn: Molly

Molly, for instance, worked for a Silicon Valley firm as a software designer. A Stanford engineering graduate who was a strong individual contributor, she was quickly identified as a rising star and soon promoted to manager. In any first leadership role, there's a lot to learn—setting objectives, giving feedback, valuing the managerial role rather than the role of an individual contributor. It was a big job for someone as young as Molly, but she threw herself into the technical problems her group faced. She was eager to prove herself, and she worked with great energy seven days a week and helped her project team overcome serious technological roadblocks. Molly received much praise and soon was promoted again.

In her new leadership role, however, Molly was stretched too thin. Her technical skill and hard work could only take her so far. The demands of the job required her to delegate and to motivate—two skills that Molly had not mastered. And she had never learned how to build and lead a team; she had succeeded in her previous managerial role through sheer technical brilliance. Now brilliance wasn't enough. She ended up driving herself and her team to the point that they burned out. One direct report quit; two others complained to Molly's boss that they were spinning their wheels, and Molly herself became distant and uncommunicative. Within eight months of this second promotion, Molly was fired. Even worse, she had learned little about herself or her weaknesses, preferring to believe that bad luck and an unappreciative management team were responsible for her demise.

Moving Toward Success: Gordon

Like Molly, Gordon had a strong technical background. Employed by an aerospace firm as an engineer, he was leading a research group working on composite materials to be used in aircraft. When his firm received an RFP to develop a composite-material wing for military aircraft, Gordon helped craft the proposal that resulted in a $1 billion assignment. Gordon was put in charge of the design team, and it was a tremendous opportunity for him; it was also the first time he had ever managed such a large project.

From the beginning, the project seemed doomed. Gordon had a terrible time staffing the project properly and getting the resources necessary from other parts of his firm. They fell behind schedule, and though Gordon worked frantically to salvage it, he couldn't do so. His firm lost millions of dollars on the failed effort, and Gordon bore the brunt of the failure. Not only did he feel like everyone in the firm blamed him for what went wrong, but local media gave such extensive coverage to the problems experienced by Gordon's firm that even Gordon's kids were taunted at school. Gordon wasn't fired, but he was moved out of the firm's main building into a small office nearby and given a minor project to work on.

At first, Gordon was furious with management and his colleagues. For several weeks, he was angry that he was given the lion's share of the blame when, in fact, it was a group failure. He thought about resigning or looking for another job. Then he decided to shift his focus. He reflected on his shortcomings as a leader and how they had contributed to the failure. He also wrote up his observations about what went wrong and shared them with others in the company. People were surprised at how insightful they were, both from management and technical perspectives.

After about a year, Gordon moved back into the main building, receiving a new assignment in part because he'd maintained a core group of supporters. Gordon didn't allow his anger to spill out and damage important relationships. After he had calmed down, he realized that he really didn't have much to be angry about. Gordon soon began giving presentations to other project managers in the firm about lessons that could be learned from his failure. A few years later, Gordon's firm received a contract to build a composite tail for a commercial airliner. Gordon's supervisor recommended him as a project leader, and this time the project came off without a hitch.

Contents of the Book

The thirteen passages discussed in this book are not necessarily the only ones that occur in the life of a leader, but they are the most common ones. As we said earlier, there is a chapter devoted to each passage, and most chapters include discussions of four topics: (1) diverse work experiences, (2) career and work adversity, (3) diverse life experiences, and (4) difficult life experiences. In each chapter, you'll find stories that bring the passages to life and tips and techniques that will help you derive maximum learning from them.

The first two chapters put the book's themes in context. We begin by defining what constitutes effective leadership today and how an individual's attitudes and actions within the passages increase or decrease the person's effectiveness. The next chapter emphasizes the importance of a learning mind-set as people make these journeys. We'll discuss how some are adept at picking up nuggets of self-knowledge, whereas others are oblivious to what is going on inside of them. To be an eager and aware learner is crucial for leaders, and we'll look at how to develop this knack for learning.

The book's last two chapters provide perspective for individuals and organizations. For individuals, the discussion suggests the traits that help leaders become good passage-makers; for organizations, it focuses on ways they can support executives who are in the midst of a passage and increase the odds that the experience facilitates their development as leaders.

In between these opening and closing chapters, you'll find thirteen predictable, intense passages. Yes, they can be emotionally draining and stressful. Yes, they can also be tremendously meaningful and thought provoking. This book will guide you through the highs and lows and help you emerge from them with greater leadership self-awareness and skill.

1
___

What Is Effective Leadership?

Sweet are the uses of adversity.
—William Shakespeare, *As You Like It*

If you want to become an effective leader, what, specifically, should you do to make that happen?

Hundreds of leadership books purport to answer this question today. Just walk into any bookstore. Broadly, the research, thinking, and writing about leadership can be divided into two camps. One camp holds that leadership is all about behavior and that if you want to excel, you should learn and replicate the key behaviors of good leaders. Many companies pursue this view by developing competency models and then rigorously assessing and training their leaders accordingly. The other camp holds that leadership is all about character, values, and authenticity, and companies that adhere to this view focus on transmitting company values and orienting leaders to the right way to do things.

Both approaches are valid—and incomplete. Most leadership development efforts that revolve around *either* character *or* behavior are only sporadically effective because of an inherent problem. Leaders emerge from training emboldened with new ideas and ways of doing things but then re-enter a company culture that has not been modified. They find it difficult to sustain their leadership effectiveness, failing to carry over their success from the learning context to the leadership context.

Consider that in recent years the leadership development

industry has exploded, yet just about every organization complains about a leadership shortage. With the increase in training programs and knowledge about this subject, logic dictates that we should be doing a better job of meeting the organizational demand for talent. In fact, most organizations bemoan the dearth of "ready now" leaders with maturity, judgment, and skill.

What's missing?

Over the years, we've taught, coached, and counseled hundreds of senior executives in Fortune 200 companies throughout the world. Leaders who do not succeed tend to be people who lack self-awareness. Daniel Goleman has made this basic truth clear by describing the importance of emotional intelligence as an important component of effective leadership. Ineffective leaders don't understand their own motivations or acknowledge their weaknesses; they don't engage in reflection, especially when they fail and are unwilling to assume accountability. As smart and skilled as these people may be, they don't really know themselves, and this lack of self-knowledge derails them, especially when they face new leadership challenges.

High-performing leaders, however, are aware of their strengths *and* their weaknesses; they talk and think about their limitations and failures and try to learn from them. They see themselves as continuously learning, adapting, and responding to both positive and negative circumstances. Most important, they are highly conscious of their feelings and behaviors as they move through life, including personal and professional passages: losing a job, being promoted, changing companies, mourning the death of a loved one, dealing with a divorce, and so on.

These passages have an impact on leaders, just as they do on all of us. If you go through them with your eyes—and your mind—closed, you diminish your own development. If you go through them consciously and are open to the lessons they hold, you dramatically increase the odds of being a consistently effective leader.

Ineffective Leadership Development

Most organizations, of course, don't look at leadership development from the perspective of these passages. Because of intense competition and the need to build a pipeline of leadership talent, many companies have recently begun to recognize the value of coaching and of conducting 360-degree assessments, as well as other self-awareness-building tools. But companies are still intensely results-driven. Leadership development tends to focus on outcomes, behaviors, competencies, cases, and skills. The reality of leadership is denied, including its self-questioning, its self-doubt, even its vulnerability. Every day, we encounter messages equating strong leadership with certainty, firmness, and the absence of self-reflection.

Explicitly or implicitly, most companies discourage people from talking about their problems or seeking help as they navigate some of the most important circumstances that affect their lives as individuals and as leaders. People may talk to their boss or coworker about the demands of work, company politics, conflict, unmet expectations, or inadequate performance. Or they may discuss specific issues that were pointed out during a performance review. But the discussions usually stay focused on action rather than feeling—on how they can solve the problem rather than face the underlying issues with which they're wrestling.

It also seems counterintuitive to confess what they see as their failings to a boss or mentor. For instance, suppose Janet is a top talent recently recruited by her boss from another company. How easily does Janet tell the person who has invested a considerable amount of the company's money and his own reputation in her that she is struggling with a new corporate culture and its policies? Figure 1.1 represents a "learning pyramid" (how people learn in an organization) graphically.

Similarly, in the senior ranks of most large companies today, discussion of significant personal experience remains a taboo. People experience all types of traumas in their lives that shape their outlook as well as their character and commitment. And they are ex-

Figure 1.1. The Learning Pyramid.

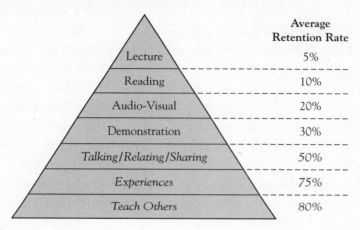

	Average Retention Rate
Lecture	5%
Reading	10%
Audio-Visual	20%
Demonstration	30%
Talking/Relating/Sharing	50%
Experiences	75%
Teach Others	80%

Source: Jeanne Meister, *Corporate Universities.*

pected to suppress discussion of these events at work. Only through coaching senior executives have we discovered how significant these personal passages can be and how much they affect, actually even shape, leadership behavior. Men especially feel as if they must tough it out and not allow trouble at home to spill over into their work. The result is that people sit on their feelings and separate their leadership role from their private self. Invariably, this chasm is projected into the work environment, creating a perception of inauthenticity and even distrust. For instance, many executives who go through a divorce deal with their pain and anger by resolving to work harder, travel more frequently, demand more from others, and take umbrage at perceived slights or criticism.

Working through the significant passages of life and career requires time and space for reflection, and companies generally don't allow people this time and space. In most companies today, people aren't allowed sabbaticals; they aren't given the opportunity to take a step back and gain perspective. They simply don't have a chance to think deeply about who they are and what they're doing. Consequently, they persevere through these passages oblivious to their impact. If they fail at work, they deny culpability for the failure. If they feel terribly sad, they force themselves to be relentlessly upbeat, optimistic, and confident.

Although this may look like effective leadership, it comes with significant costs. When leaders aren't in touch with who they are and what they feel, they are ineffective as leaders. They do not convey passion, power, or persuasion. They may reject feedback, fail to see the negative consequences of their actions, respond poorly to stress, or miss important relationship signals from others. And more often than not, all this gets taken out on their organizations. Perhaps most significantly, they don't deal well with change. Only when people know themselves, acknowledge their experiences and feelings, and confront their humanity do they demonstrate resilience and the capacity to adapt.

Leadership Development That Includes Learning from Passages

The good news is that the passages can serve as a career roadmap. If you're aware of what the passages are and how to go through them, you'll learn and grow from each experience. And this constitutes effective leadership development. To understand how this leadership learning and growth takes place, let's look at a 2 × 2 matrix (Figure 1.2) that puts it in perspective.

Contrary to the conventional wisdom, the matrix shows that there's more to leadership development than taking on a variety of work challenges. Although work diversity is one quadrant of the matrix, the other three are equally important. Some companies today are beginning to acknowledge that failure is a powerful teacher. The best leaders experience job and career setbacks and learn from them; they grieve and integrate the lessons learned from personal failures and tragedies, and they make an effort to live a life filled with a wide range of people, places, and events.

The combination of diversity and adversity, cross-hatched with personal and professional experiences, drives leadership learning

Figure 1.2. Leadership Learning.

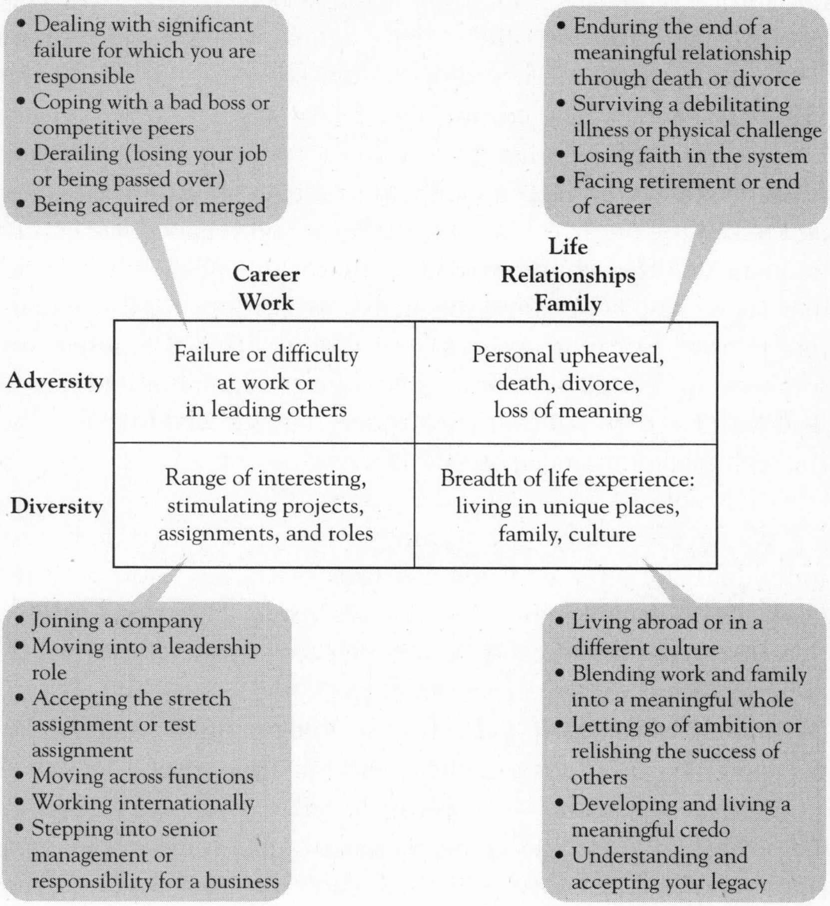

- Dealing with significant failure for which you are responsible
- Coping with a bad boss or competitive peers
- Derailing (losing your job or being passed over)
- Being acquired or merged

- Enduring the end of a meaningful relationship through death or divorce
- Surviving a debilitating illness or physical challenge
- Losing faith in the system
- Facing retirement or end of career

	Career **Work**	**Life** **Relationships** **Family**
Adversity	Failure or difficulty at work or in leading others	Personal upheaval, death, divorce, loss of meaning
Diversity	Range of interesting, stimulating projects, assignments, and roles	Breadth of life experience: living in unique places, family, culture

- Joining a company
- Moving into a leadership role
- Accepting the stretch assignment or test assignment
- Moving across functions
- Working internationally
- Stepping into senior management or responsibility for a business

- Living abroad or in a different culture
- Blending work and family into a meaningful whole
- Letting go of ambition or relishing the success of others
- Developing and living a meaningful credo
- Understanding and accepting your legacy

and growth. More specifically, it's a leader's willingness to reflect, face into, and talk about what he's going through that facilitates his development. Unfortunately, many companies don't encourage reflection, conversation, and openness. The personal side of the matrix is generally ignored, and job adversity, especially any type of failure, is viewed with disapproval. In succession-planning discussions or promotion decisions, failure, setbacks, and reversals are entered on the negative side of the ledger. And yet good leaders fail frequently. Although some of these failures are public and spectacular, such as a CEO missing the analyst projections for three quarters in row, many are private and partial. It's not unusual for someone to do well with one aspect of an assignment and not so well with another. For example, leaders may succeed in mastering the technical or financial aspects of their job but fail to develop or engage people.

We have learned from coaching many senior leaders that some individuals are often continuously promoted; they show outward evidence of success but feel like failures inside. They don't believe they deserve success because of their perceived inadequacies or self-criticism. And in every organization, you'll find leaders who are very successful professionally and very miserable personally, and the gap between their two lives is gradually eroding their spirit.

At times of adversity, people experience teachable moments. These are windows for learning, for making quantum leaps in emotional intelligence. The individual who enjoys one success after another may become very proficient at what she does but will never grow much as a leader. The person who has some adversity mixed with the success, however, will gain insights that translate eventually into effectiveness.

When you struggle with a stretch assignment, for instance, you have the chance to analyze what's behind this struggle. Perhaps you're not prepared to handle a task that calls for you to function in an ambiguous environment. Maybe you're finding that you're missing a skill that's necessary for the assignment. If you reflect and talk about the situation and are open to revealing where you're coming up short, you'll acquire self-knowledge that will serve you well in the future. You'll work at functioning more effectively amid ambiguity or at acquiring the missing skill, and the next time you need it, you'll either have it or you'll realize that you need to find someone else to help you.

Although everyone experiences adversity and diversity in unique ways, the general nature of these experiences can be predicted and prepared for. When you know the passages you will encounter, you're better able to maximize their value as learning tools. As you may have noticed when looking at the list of passages, they're organized according to the four quadrants of the matrix: (1) diversity of work experiences, (2) work adversity, (3) diversity of life experiences, and (4) life adversity. To give you a sense of how these passages can benefit a leader, let's look at the experience of one fast-track executive who was derailed by someone he considered a bad boss.

A Bad Boss as Potential Derailer

Phil had "star" written all over him from the time he graduated with honors from a top MBA program. Handsome, smart, charismatic, and the son of a business school professor to boot, Phil joined a major packaged-goods firm after graduating and quickly was given increasing amounts of responsibility and a series of promotions. Not only did he meet or exceed expectations in his first three positions but he was fortunate to have the types of bosses who came from backgrounds similar to his and with whom he quickly established good relationships.

Then Phil was transferred to a new group, and this time his boss was Tony, a tough guy who had never received an advanced degree. Tony had achieved his position in the company through hard work and hard-won expertise; he was street smart and knew how to deal with organizational politics. From the moment Tony set eyes on

Phil, he seemed to have it in for him, or at least that was Phil's perception. He threw verbal jabs at Phil whenever he cited a famous business guru or theory as justification for an action. Tony told Phil that he'd reached a rung on the ladder where his education and charm didn't mean anything. Even worse, he consistently rejected Phil's ideas and kept him off teams "where the real action was." He told Phil he had a lot to learn before he could play with the tough competition.

Phil was furious and immediately convinced himself that Tony had it in for him because he was jealous of Phil's privileged background. When Tony would tell him what he had done wrong—and he'd usually tell him bluntly and coarsely—Phil tuned out. He was certain that Tony had nothing of value to pass on and that sooner or later he'd find another position far away from Tony.

Phil was right, at least in the sense that he would be able to find another job. He took an offer from one of his company's competitors, but he quickly ran into problems with a boss who was a woman. Phil told friends that her unwillingness to give him a promotion he deserved was based on her hatred of all men. After a few months, he went over his new boss's head and was able to finagle a transfer to another unit. Though he got along all right with his new boss, his performance was mediocre, and he seemed unable to recapture his old star quality.

Phil's problem was that he was oblivious to the passage of "dealing with a bad boss." Whether Tony actually was a bad boss is beside the point. Phil simply didn't use his problems with Tony for reflection and conversation and for being open about his own weaknesses. If he had, he might have realized that he had a problem dealing with people from different backgrounds, that he was overly reliant on his charm and education, and that he didn't put in the time and effort necessary to do certain assignments well. If he had become more conscious of his shortcomings, he might have been better prepared to deal with them when they surfaced in the future.

A Test of Learning from Passages

The odds are that you've gone through at least a few of the thirteen passages we outline. We would like you to consider *how* you traversed a passage. Here is a list of the passages:

- Joining a company
- Moving into a leadership role
- Accepting the stretch assignment
- Assuming responsibility for a business
- Dealing with significant failure for which you are responsible
- Coping with a bad boss and competitive peers
- Losing your job or being passed over for promotion
- Being part of an acquisition or merger
- Living in a different country or culture
- Finding a meaningful balance between work and family
- Letting go of ambition
- Facing personal upheaval
- Losing faith in the system

Choose one passage from this list that you've gone through. Ideally, pick one that you experienced relatively recently and that had a significant impact on your personal or professional life. Based on this particular passage, answer the following questions:

When you were going through this experience, did you have much time to step away from it and think long and hard about what was occurring?

After the event that constitutes the passage had ended, did you reflect on what had taken place? Did you put this event into the larger context of your life (work or personal) and attempt to figure out its meaning in the greater scheme of things?

Did you engage at least one other person in conversation about this passage? Was this conversation confined to the problem and possible solutions (what happened and what you might do about it), or did you talk about deeper issues: how it made you feel, your fears, your expectations?

If the event had an adverse consequence, did you admit to yourself or others how you may have failed or come up short?

Is there anything you learned from this passage? Motivate you to reassess certain assumptions? Make you aware of a vulnerability? Motivate you to acquire a specific knowledge or skill? Prepare you to handle a similar passage better in the future?

If you're like most people, you answered no to at least some of these questions. Perhaps, like Phil, you became defensive when you failed and blamed your problems on others as you went through the passage. Perhaps you simply rushed through it, anxious to get it behind you and avoid dealing with the issues it raised. Most of us lack the time, energy, and inclination to go through these passages consciously and deeply. Consider, though, that the benefit of doing so is greater leadership effectiveness.

When we think about being more effective as a leader, we generally don't think about developing greater self-awareness or emotional intelligence. Instead, we think in classic terms about what makes an effective leader. We believe we need to acquire certain skills—decision making, strategizing, and so on—to become a strong leader. Or we are convinced that winning is key and that if we just become better at getting things done and achieving results, we'll increase our effectiveness. Or we work at our people skills, recognizing that leadership is increasingly about building strong relationships.

All of this is fine, except that these actions provide only incremental gains in leadership effectiveness. Ultimately, the way we use our skills, obtain results, or establish relationships is contingent on our internal awareness of who we are. If we're blind to our weak spots, they're bound to trip us up. We may be a great relationship builder under ideal circumstances, but under stress our weaknesses surface and we destroy a critical relationship. Because we're not aware, we don't learn from experience, especially the critical passage experiences.

This brings up the key question: How do the passages help us learn what we need to know to become effective leaders? We hope that this book will allow you to answer that question successfully.

2

How Do Leaders Learn?

To answer the question posed in this chapter title and to understand how the passages facilitate leadership learning and growth, we need to define our terms. There are two major categories of leadership learning: (1) classroom learning and (2) experience-based learning. Classroom learning, as the name implies, focuses on cognitive understanding, on absorbing case histories, and listening to other people share their knowledge. Although executives need to know certain theories and facts in order to improve their performance, committing data to memory may not actually influence leadership behavior, especially emotional intelligence, which cannot be acquired in a linear, cognitive setting.

The second type of learning is experience-based—what you learn by doing. Although experts differ on how people learn from experience, all seem to agree that learning involves a change in behavior relative to the individual's interaction with the environment. Typically, you have an experience, then you reflect on it and talk about it; your awareness of what you're thinking and feeling then changes how you lead, better preparing you for the next experience.

But are all experiences useful in the same way? As you'll recall, it's the *mix* of adverse, diverse, professional, and personal experi-

Note: We are indebted to the work of our colleague Ronald Heifetz of Harvard University for his insights about technical and adaptive work.

ences that catalyzes effective leadership. Repeating the same narrow range of experiences won't do much good, even if they are successful. Although significant passages provide the needed mix of experience, not everyone learns equally well when going through the passages. To understand why some people emerge from a passage as wiser, more effective leaders and others don't, we need to know a little about what goes on in people's minds when they're confronted with new learning.

How Attitude Affects Learning

One way to understand the impact of experiential learning is through programs we have developed such as CDR International Action Learning. Leaders range broadly across a continuum from being open to new experiences to being closed; they integrate experience into preconceived ideas and opinions.

Events can be categorized as routine or repetitive (those not requiring new learning or solvable with a technical solution) or as adaptive (those requiring new ways of responding, behaving, or problem solving). See Figure 2.1 for an explanation of why some experiences are so much richer than others in terms of their learning potential.

At the top of this matrix, two attitudes are represented. In the open-minded mode, people go into a new situation without feeling

Figure 2.1. The Learning Potential of Experiences.

	Open	Closed
Adaptive (needs new learning)	Big Opportunity	Missed Opportunity
Technical (needs no new learning)	Limited Opportunity	No Opportunity

that they already know how to respond or handle it; they formulate a theory or new assumptions *as a result of the experience*. In the closed attitude, people go into a new situation looking to fit it into a preconceived theory or set of assumptions.

On the left side of the matrix, the two descriptions relate to whether a given situation demands new learning (adaptive change) or, if no new learning is needed (technical change), to deal effectively with the situation.

If you're in the Big Opportunity quadrant, you're stretching yourself, integrating new ideas, and possibly changing your view of yourself. Stretch assignments, promotions, and the passages we describe in this book can all constitute big opportunities. There's plenty new to learn here, and you'll take advantage of the situation by thinking about and doing things in new ways. You'll pay attention to negative feedback about your behaviors and consider changing them.

If you're in the Missed Opportunity quadrant, you'll sabotage your learning. You won't listen to negative feedback, and you may even deny that you have any problem or weakness, despite evidence to the contrary. You'll persist in doing things the way you've always done them. Leaders who preside over declining businesses, for example, face strong adaptive challenges but build their strategy based on past successes.

If you're in the Limited Opportunity quadrant, your open-minded attitude will benefit you, but the challenge will not require maximum effort on your part. You're probably doing assignments that you've done successfully in the past, creating the illusion of accomplishment but relying on familiar problem-solving approaches and routines. Leaders who have been in the same position for a number of years frequently fall into this quadrant: competent, even expert, but not growing.

If you're in the No Opportunity quadrant, you're a prisoner of your experience. Your negative attitude, combined with routine assignments, will stifle your leadership development. Burned-out or rusted-out leaders who have experienced frequent downsizings, been passed over for promotion, or developed a cynical shell define their leadership role in narrow terms and accompany that with a closed mind.

In the life of a leader, moving into the Big Opportunity quadrant can be difficult. You're constrained not only by the assignments you're given but by your attitude and history. If you're like most successful executives, you find it difficult to acknowledge, both to yourself and others, that you're not the all-knowing, all-seeing, always-confident leader you feel you're supposed to be.

Another way to view this process is through a theory first posited by psychologist David Kolb. He developed a theory of learning (now referred to as the Kolb learning theory; see Figure 2.2) that illustrates the learning process and underlies much of the theory about how people learn and develop.

Kolb's theory posits that after you have an experience, you reflect on that experience and derive meaning from it. Based on this meaning, you form concepts about things such as your organization, your leadership, and yourself. You essentially create your own "theory of the case" to explain how things work in a given situation. After you form this theory of the case, you test it to determine its validity. If you find it's valid, you've learned something new.

Figure 2.2. Kolb's Learning Model.

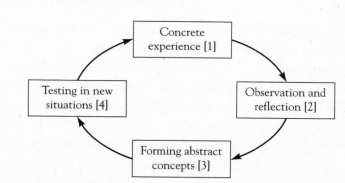

Source: Adapted from Kolb, 1984.

If, however, you have a know-it-all attitude, you'll rarely form new concepts and theories or test them out. Instead, you'll encounter a situation, assume that it's just like all the other situations you've successfully dealt with, and use the same thought processes and methods you used in the past. And in many instances, you'll fail.

Failure as a Second Chance

Failure, though, gives you a second chance to learn. Failure of any kind always tells you something about yourself. It grabs your attention and, if you can remain nondefensive, suggests that perhaps you don't know something you need to know. Unfortunately, many people don't capitalize on this second chance to learn. In working with many large global companies, we can say unequivocally that organizations aren't fond of failure. A powerful learning opportunity is therefore denied, diminished, or deducted. Most large companies don't give leaders the time to reflect on the experience or the permission to admit their vulnerabilities. In the wake of business failure, mistake, error, or disappointment, many leaders deny (to themselves and others) their own role. CEOs account for disappointing earnings by blaming "unexpected circumstances." Senior executives cite the weather, consumer behavior, currency fluctuation, pricing, unruly competitors, or some other external event as a logical explanation for negative outcomes. No leader ever says, "I screwed up."

If you aspire to obtain a top leadership position, however, you can't continually scapegoat and deny your failures. Through coaching many successful, accomplished leaders, we have observed that personal accountability differentiates learners from laggards. Acknowledging and expressing the negative feelings that accompany failure opens the door to change.

In leadership development programs, we frequently cite the SARA (Shock, Anger, Rejection, Acceptance) model to describe the four emotional reactions leaders experience in encountering situations or outcomes they don't like:

1. *Shock:* You acknowledge your surprise that you messed up, others don't like you, or you failed to meet your own or others' expectations.

2. *Anger:* You are furious that things didn't go according to plan.

3. *Rejection:* You blame someone or something for events and reject the information or your role in creating the outcome.

4. *Acceptance:* You accept your vulnerability and acknowledge that failure and your feelings are part of being human.

Dealing with these feelings can be difficult if you're left to your own devices. Let's look at how the passages can help you deal with them effectively and facilitate learning.

Ways to Create a New Identity

In one sense, "leadership learning" is counterintuitive. In *The Leadership Pipeline*, Jim Noel, along with coauthors Ram Charan and Steve Drotter, suggests that executives make "turns" in the pipeline—from individual contributor to manager, for instance—based on their success in their previous job. Each turn requires new skills, values, and use of time, as well as significant adaptation to a new role (see Figure 2.3). The individual contributor's skill as a salesperson earned him a promotion to sales manager, but the skills required for a managerial position are different from those of an individual contributor. Nonetheless, he still relies on the salesperson skills that brought him success in the past. This is

> When I faced myself in the mirror, I realized that Honeywell was changing me more than I was changing Honeywell. I thought I was making a difference, but it wasn't the kind of difference I wanted to make.
>
> BILL GEORGE, FORMER CHAIRMAN AND CEO, MEDTRONIC

Figure 2.3. The Leadership Pipeline.

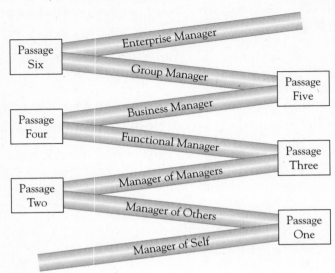

Source: Charan, Drotter, and Noel, 2001.

perfectly natural, but it will prevent him from learning and growing as a manager. His instinct will be to rely on what he knows and
to avoid tasks that require what he doesn't know.

People often go through the passages relying on behaviors and
attitudes that served them well in the past. The passages, though,
challenge your self-definition ("I'm always successful" or "I'm usually in control"). Undertaking a stretch assignment, living abroad,
mourning the death of a loved one, or dealing with a bad boss all
communicate to people that "you're not in Kansas anymore." It's
difficult to ignore the signs that life has changed and that you need
to change with them. Of course, some people do ignore the signs.
But each passage presents a new opportunity to learn and grow, and
if you see it as such, you can dramatically improve your leadership
effectiveness.

Learning from a passage, however, isn't possible unless you let
go of your past assumptions. In other words, you must admit that

some of the very attributes, qualities, attitudes, and skills that made you successful in the past won't necessarily make you successful in the future and that your old knowledge may no longer be applicable. Such an admission makes you vulnerable; you feel exposed as a novice after enjoying your role as an experienced pro. This is a tough psychological transition, especially because you may not even be aware the transition is taking place. In coaching senior executives who encounter a significant passage, we encourage them to admit their vulnerability as the precursor to learning.

Typically, you're so caught up in the excitement of a passage or the complex issues it raises that learning from it is the last thing on your mind. For instance, you've just been given the task of turning a business around—a business that's critical to the company's future. Weighed down with high expectations and excited about proving yourself, you feel you need to be the expert right from the start, that you must hit the ground running. As a result, you plunge into the assignment, focused only on getting it done rather than stepping back and figuring out what you really need to know to do the assignment effectively and how you can maximize your first months in the new role. Companies such as Dell and Johnson & Johnson are beginning to intervene at this point and help leaders with this passage through transition coaching, but usually they don't do that. Leaders may receive advice from bosses or mentors, but the advice is usually technical in nature, confined to achieving the task set before them. It's only when things don't go well that they begin to receive the feedback they really need.

> I learned a lot about leadership in turnaround situations. This is an especially good leadership experience: to not know everything and to be highly dependent on other people for good learning. In my prior environment, I made almost all the calls myself and didn't need any team input. But in the new, current environment, even if you are already an expert, it is a mistake not to ask other people.
>
> THOMAS EBELING, CEO, NOVARTIS PHARMACEUTICALS

To maximize learning in each passage, be willing to give up your identity. For instance, this could mean no longer defining yourself as a star, a winner, or super-achiever. The process of evolving one's identity is often unconscious and subtle and occurs over a period of time. But it is central to the process of learning. It may mean no longer wrapping your identity around your spouse (if you go through a divorce) or in terms of your home or neighbors (when you move to another state or country). Only letting go of the old identity makes it possible to forge a new one—as a manager, a single person, or a resident of a foreign country. To forge this identity, you'll need to acquire new skills and beliefs, and this acquisition is central to the learning process.

Example of Adversity as a Spur to Learning

Andrew was a technological wizard—a brilliant guy who did well as an MIS executive at a Fortune 100 company and someone we encountered in a recent leadership development program. In certain ways, Andrew was the prototypical high-tech leader. He loved nothing better than spending time immersing himself in software design, emerging from behind his computer screen only to bounce ideas off other technically savvy colleagues. As sharp as he was, Andrew didn't establish any strong relationships at work. It wasn't that he was antisocial; he just was so goal-oriented that he didn't feel compelled to have lengthy conversations about anything but work. As a result, people often felt that Andrew used them—milked them for knowledge and then ignored them on more personal matters.

One unbelievable day, Andrew was in a severe auto accident that left him partially paralyzed. For the next six months, lucky to be alive, he recuperated and rehabbed. At first, Andrew was depressed. He had worked nonstop since graduating from college, and his partial paralysis and rehabilitation prevented him from returning to work. Even worse, he couldn't work on the computer because both his wrists had been broken, and nerve damage made it difficult for him to type. It was a terribly frustrating time, and Andrew was filled with self-doubt and pity.

Gradually, he emerged from his funk. As part of the rehab process, he met other people with various injuries and began communicating with them on an emotional level; they talked about their fears and their hopes for the future. He joined a support group that served not only as a clearinghouse of information for people with severe injuries but paved the way for friendships with a variety of people outside the high-tech world. After Andrew regained most of his wrist function and returned to work, he found himself much more willing to talk with and listen to others. Though he still loved designing software, he was much more willing to help others when they were having problems with their designs. Before his accident, Andrew was never considered a candidate for team manager, despite his technical skills. After his return to work, however, he was promoted to this position because he had learned to relate to people in ways that fostered their development. Andrew's organization considered emotional intelligence a critical leadership skill, and when he clearly had acquired it, it made him a prime candidate for managing the team.

Andrew was forced to learn because of the adversity he unexpectedly encountered. He took advantage of the learning available in his passage. Through reflection and conversations, he learned a lot about himself, helping him create a new, more effective identity.

The Value of Failure

In the broadest sense of the term, Andrew failed when he experienced partial paralysis. Specifically, his body failed, and at that time all his skills and knowledge were inadequate to deal with what he was going through. Andrew could have chosen to become stuck in his failure, and for many leaders whose careers do not unfold according to their own plans and prescriptions, remaining stuck is an unfortunate outcome. Andrew could have remained bitter about the bad luck that caused him to be at the wrong place at the wrong time. Instead, he opened himself up to new people and possibilities. His failure was a catalyst for change and growth.

Most people who move through life experiencing one success after another are shallow. In fact, as professional coaches we can often quickly distinguish between senior executives who have encountered and overcome failure and those who have continually ascended the corporate hierarchy with no detours or unplanned stops. Without a failure or two along the way, leaders never have to move out of their comfort zones, adjust their identities, or develop their capacity for compassion. This isn't to say that failure is fun or should be sought. Failing hurts. Too much of it can damage your career or, more important, your life.

Failure, though, can also deepen you. It gives you a sense of your own fallibility and forces you to reassess your point of view. As Andrew discovered, increased empathy is a common byproduct of failure. You can gain key relationship-building skills that you'd never acquire if your life were failure-free.

Because failure is a recurring theme in the passages we're about to discuss, we want to be sure you understand how failure helps you learn. To that end, try the following exercise:

1. Identify something significant you failed at in your personal or professional life. It can be anything from a marriage to a job. Be specific about the failure. Summarize the failure in a sentence, and use the word *fail*:

   I was one of three candidates for the general manager position at my company, but I *failed* to be selected.

   I *failed* as a father to my teenaged son because I pushed him too hard and hurt the relationship.

2. Describe how you felt about the failure immediately after it occurred. Did you blame others for the failure? Did you act like the world had come to an end? Did you question your ability or intelligence?

3. Now move forward in time. Using hindsight, list any positive outcomes from the failure. Include any positives in the following categories:

Skills you acquired

Lessons you learned

Relationships you established

4. Identify how the failure may have changed you as a person. Specify traits or attitudes that you developed as a result of the failure. Do a before-and-after portrait of yourself, and note whether the "after" portrait represents a wiser, more mature person.

Most people recognize the value of failure only months or years later. Senior executives are often comfortable publicly discussing their failures that happened two years ago but not two days ago. Our goal is help you to recognize it in "real time," so that when you're going through the passage, you can capitalize on its ability to help you learn and grow as a leader.

3

Joining a Company

On the surface, this passage—the first we describe—may appear to be relatively simple when you first embark on it. After all, you join a company because the company wants you. Your new organization welcomes you with open arms. There is a deceptive sense of smooth sailing, but if you're not prepared for the storms ahead, you will be sunk.

It helps to remember that this passage is a transition and, as with all transitions, a gap exists between appearance and reality. Or to put it more bluntly, what you see is often not what you get. This is true for recent graduates and even more so for veteran executives. According to research done many years ago by Harvard psychologist David McClelland, individuals are motivated by needs for achievement, power, and affiliation that vary throughout the life cycle. For example, teenagers are often motivated by their need for acceptance by their peers—a strong need for affiliation that carries over into college and first jobs. Younger people entering a corporation for the first time are motivated by a need to belong, to be included, to be on the team. They want to fit in with a company and a culture. After a while, these new recruits begin to establish a professional reputation and to focus on achieving career goals. Eventually, after being promoted, a need for power and impact comes into play. See Figure 3.1 for a "motive profile."

Figure 3.1. Motive Profile.

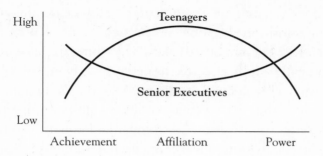

Source: Bridges, 1980.

Joining a company at the outset of a career can sometimes result in disappointment when young people discover that their values don't match those of their new companies and they must compromise or leave. People joining new companies at midcareer may be similarly frustrated to discover that, despite promised opportunities for achievement or promotion, not everyone is eager to have them on board; they sometimes encounter resistance or outright hostility from employees who resent that an outsider was hired, perhaps for a job they thought was rightfully theirs.

Even more problematic for veteran executives is their attitude; they join companies brimming with confidence and certainty that they know exactly what to do. As we've discussed, their previous success frequently makes them closed to new learning. As a result, top people join companies believing they have been hired to make change, improve performance, and rewrite history, and conclude that they must know everything necessary to succeed. And then they fail.

Like every passage, joining a company contains formidable obstacles, as well as tremendous opportunities for leadership learning and growth. To take advantage of these opportunities, you need to understand why this passage can turn dark and difficult in a matter of weeks or months.

Leaving Cultures and Networks

Organizations and individuals often underestimate the difficulty of making the transition from one company to the next. When companies spend a lot of money to make a major hire, they assume that this person will be fully effective from day one. Even though they may grant him a brief period of adjustment—usually no more than three months—they expect their recruited high-performer to provide a fast return on investment. Companies frequently assume as well that because this senior leader has been so successful elsewhere, he'll pick things up quickly and need little hand-holding before he starts delivering on his promise.

The individual, too, joins a new organization with great confidence that things will work out well. She fully expects that she will be able to match or exceed her earlier performance. She figures that if she works hard and draws on her past experience and expertise, success is a given.

In reality, both the organization and the individual are in for rude awakenings. According to the research of two of our colleagues, Dan Ciampa and Michael Watkins, authors of the seminal

---

There's a certain point in everyone's life when you must look at yourself in the mirror and ask, "Am I what I want to be or am I becoming something else that this organization wants me to be?" You have to decide if you are going to sell out to the organization and become what it wants you to be. In that sense, you lose some major parts of yourself. It's not overnight. It's like stone that erodes as water washes over it over time and smoothes its sharp edges. I think that's the process by which some people eventually sell out to the company. Then ten years later, they wake up and they say, "Now I can't get out. I've got kids in college, university; I'm stuck and I can't get out of this. I'll just go for early retirement.

BILL GEORGE, FORMER CHAIRMAN AND CEO, MEDTRONIC

---

book *Right From the Start,* when people join companies, they immediately lose two resources from their old companies:

1. *An understanding of the culture:* They knew how to deal with its unwritten rules and biases in order to get things done.
2. *A network:* They had established relationships with people who could help them obtain information, ideas, money, and talent to overcome obstacles and achieve objectives.

Establishing these two resources in a new company takes time; without them, even the smartest, most accomplished leaders can flounder.

This problem is exacerbated when executives come from companies with strong cultures. Articles have documented the failures of top executives from General Electric when they leave to join other organizations. Most recently, *Wall Street Journal* articles have detailed some of the difficulties that former GE senior executive Bob Nardelli has encountered as CEO of Home Depot. According to published reports, he has attempted to impose GE solutions on Home Depot problems, assuming that what worked in the past will work in the present. What he hasn't anticipated is that the imposition of this style would anger some veteran Home Depot employees. If Nardelli isn't fully aware of the Home Depot culture and hasn't established a strong network, this could account for the problems he's been having.

It's not surprising that Nardelli has encountered difficulties. In working with many companies, we have observed how many former GE leaders find the passage of joining another company to be challenging. At GE, from the moment they join, employees are steeped in the culture. New hires go through a formal orientation process that indoctrinates them about the company's values, and the indoctrination process continues in more subtle ways throughout their tenure. Processes, systems, financial controls, audits, and other sophisticated management tools and techniques surrounded them at GE, which doesn't happen often at other companies.

To make a successful transition, people need to unlearn some of what they know and learn what they don't know. It's very difficult to unlearn lessons taught by successful companies such as GE, however. Strong cultures provide rule systems that implicitly govern behavior and decision making. And not just at GE. Successful companies become adept at instilling their norms and values, using everything from formal training to individual mentoring to promotions and terminations. When joining a company, people often undergo a rite of passage that's akin to joining a tribe.

> In looking for companies, you don't just go to the most prestigious companies. Go to the ones where there is an alignment of your values and focus with the company's values and purpose. That's hard to discern in advance but, as I say, you have to work hard at it. Honeywell had good values, but the way it operated you pretty much checked your values at the door. Your feelings and emotions fell on the downside.
>
> BILL GEORGE, FORMER CHAIRMAN
> AND CEO, MEDTRONIC

Although this rite tends to be carried out informally in the United States, in Japan it is a formal process. In Japan, the first day in April is the traditional starting date for new college graduates to begin their careers. At one company we observed, graduates gathered in a conference room, dressed immaculately and similarly. The management team then entered in a grand procession. The chairman of the company welcomed the new hires in a formal address, and each member of the management group arose and passed on a piece of "wisdom" to the rookies. Each of the new people was then summoned by name to the front of the room, and each had to recite an oath of allegiance. We were told this was just the start of a six-month induction process. If this is the process used in most Japanese companies, it's no wonder that people have intense affiliation with their organizations and rarely change companies.

Although companies in the United States and Europe generally don't have such a formalized induction process, their orientation still encourages affiliation and identification with the company. The programs and policies that encourage affiliation—from company meetings and parties to rewards and recognitions to morale-building training sessions—bond employees to their employers. Even though they leave for other jobs much more readily than in Japan, they still retain what they've been taught. It's not surprising, therefore, that when people go through this passage and run into resistance from individuals at their new company, they say, "When I was with my old company, this was how we handled X." Not only does this reliance on past learning prevent them from learning anything new but it annoys fellow employees. Even the highest of high-potentials can get stuck in this passage, learning little that will help them succeed in their new company and grow as a leader.

Facilitating the Journey

Ideally, organizations recognize that people need assistance when they join up, especially if they're experienced executives who have been successful at companies with strong cultures. Ideally, they offer recently hired executives coaching, as well as transition programs that make them aware of the challenges they'll face. Perhaps most significant, companies are now expecting leaders to assist their direct reports with problems they may have and intervene if they seem closed to acquiring new and necessary values and skills.

The odds are, though, that bosses won't do much to help because of the pace of business, the difficulty of giving feedback to senior colleagues, and the expectation that someone successful elsewhere must know what he's doing. People in senior leadership positions, especially, struggle with finding the balance between trying to extinguish culturally inappropriate behavior in new hires and valuing it. Senior executives, in particular, tend to assume that other senior executives appreciate autonomy, control, and noninterference in order to succeed, and they expect a new senior-level hire will learn the ropes on his own.

Organizations change this assumption, though, when they discover the real costs of failing to help newcomers with this passage.

In Brad Smart's book *Top Grading,* he examined senior hires at fifteen organizations and found that 50 percent of them had departed within the first two years. The cost of losing senior people is enormous. Not only are the losses financial (from money spent recruiting them) but they cause mounting anxiety and frustration within the company. When top people are heavily recruited and offered significant salaries and bonus packages, and then proceed to initiate new projects and create expectations among people who work with them and depart within two years, it affects morale as well as business results.

Companies therefore need to be proactive in helping their new executives deal with this passage; the first thing they should do is counsel them on the implicit rules of the culture and how to maximize the impact of their entry and minimize the cultural upheaval. We have been asked by many companies such as Dell, Washington Mutual, Avon, and Novartis to help accelerate the transition and learning of newly hired executives through intensive coaching and assessment. The financial investment in identifying, recruiting, rewarding, and terminating a senior-level executive in most companies today easily warrants an investment in accelerating their adaptation and learning. In designing and delivering senior-level executive programs for many global companies, CDR International has compiled a list of the top ten most common cultural mistakes executives make, which we have observed in advising and teaching hundreds of executives around the world. We've found this list to be an awareness-raising tool, spotlighting the behaviors and attitudes that prevent learning and growth in each passage. Here is the list:

1. Staying too isolated from customers, colleagues, and the market
2. Attempting too much, too fast
3. Having unrealistic expectations for performance
4. Coming in with "the answer"
5. Failing to develop good sources of information and political intelligence

6. Not aligning with the boss or his priorities

7. Not taking action quickly enough

8. Not dealing with resistance

9. Not recognizing individual differences in transitioning from one era to another

10. Failing to understand "the way things work around here"

Failing to understand the way things work and coming in with the answer are two mistakes particularly relevant to this passage. Overconfident, successful people are especially vulnerable to these mistakes, and they often believe their skills are such that they don't need to worry about how things work. Because they had the answer at their previous company, they believe they have the answer at their new one.

If you find yourself thinking this way, take stock immediately. Remind yourself that you really don't know how things work or what the answers are in this particular situation. Reflect on and talk about what you don't know. During the first few months on the job, most people will give you leave to ask dumb questions and admit you don't have a clue—this is often referred to as "idiosyncrasy credits"; you are given a limited amount of credit at the beginning to be different, stand out, and make change happen. Take advantage of this brief period of transition to be open about your lack of knowledge or skills.

More specifically, follow this five-step method to learn and grow as you move through the passage:

1. *Identify the gap between the company's intention and your experience.* During the recruiting process, senior management or a recruiter may have painted a picture of your job responsibilities or objectives that does not jibe with reality. Determine the elements of this gap and what you need to do to close it. Is your budget too small to get the job done? Do you lack the people you need? What is your real mandate for change? Is your background and skill set poorly matched to what the company wants you to accomplish?

2. *Focus on your boss and learn to read him accurately.* When you join a company, your boss can be your lifeline, connecting you to the learning you need. Let him know if you're struggling and engage in conversations with him about why. Instead of trying to impress him with your ideas and experiences, listen to what he requires of you and how he thinks you can achieve it. Most important, recognize that your boss also has priorities and a leadership agenda, and work to help him fulfill it.

3. *Build a coalition that stretches throughout the organization.* No matter how smart you are or how experienced, you can't navigate this passage alone. This network will not only help you get things done but will provide you with rich sources of learning. (See *Unnatural Leadership* by David Dotlich and Peter Cairo for more hints on "connecting" rather than "creating everything yourself.")

4. *Diagnose the culture yourself.* Don't rely on the informal grapevine or what you've read about your new company (or what the recruiter told you). If you do, you'll make assumptions that will probably be faulty. More than one executive has failed because he arrogantly assumed he "got" his new company when in reality he hadn't taken the time to reflect on what it really was all about. Reflect, talk to others, and then diagnose what makes the culture tick. Quickly developing sources of insight and information, especially about the culture, determines success for newly hired leaders.

5. *Create a time-focused vision of what you want to accomplish.* As a newcomer, you're on probation. Although your bosses will cut you some slack initially, they'll expect you to perform within a reasonable timeframe. Therefore, identify what needs to be accomplished and determine when it's best to demonstrate that you're learning, growing, and producing.

Thomas Ebeling, the CEO of Novartis's pharmaceutical division (and one of our colleagues), put many of these actions into practice as he moved from consumer-products companies like Pepsi-Cola to Novartis. Thomas arrived at Novartis with a reputation for being a driving, ruthlessly focused leader. In consumer-products companies, his approach was highly effective. Novartis, however, is like most pharmaceutical companies—a conservative and compassionate culture combined with scientific decision making. If Thomas had joined Novartis and implemented the same gung-ho style and tactics, he certainly would have failed. Instead, he has been highly successful, with four straight years of outstanding results. His success is attributable to his willingness to unlearn and learn. He transformed himself into a better listener, a more team-oriented and empathic leader; after intense study of the business, he realized that this was the type of leader the business called for.

Learning a Critical Leadership Lesson

Admitting *what you don't know* when you join a company presents a challenge to executives with healthy egos and the strong self-confidence needed to persevere, but consider the learning that results when you're open to the lessons this passage holds. First, it gives you the chance to practice broadening your network and your understanding of corporate cultures—skills that will serve you well in every leadership position you hold. The art of adapting to new cultures and building new networks is one that many executives don't practice, especially if they've spent much of their work life in only one or two companies. The skill of adaptation, however, applies to many contexts and relationships, including customers, employees, and partners.

Second, it makes you psychologically stronger, providing you with the capacity to rebound when you face the adversity that comes in other passages. Time and again, we've heard executives complain soon after joining a company, "This is the worst decision I've ever made." They often become trapped in a cycle of remorse, beating themselves up over having made what seems like a terrible move. When executives become stuck in this cycle, they don't learn and often leave. They stop trusting their instincts and start wasting their energy on self-recrimination. They may actually join a new company but leave their self-concept behind in their previous organization.

When you join a new company, expect to have a certain amount of buyer's remorse. Accept it as an opportunity to challenge your assumptions and learn a new approach to leadership. In the worst case, if the new job doesn't work out, you'll be that much better prepared for the next new company passage; you'll have developed the resilience necessary to learn in the midst of adversity. If the job does work out, you'll have demonstrated your ability to adapt to new people, policies, and environments—a trait that your company and you will value now and in the future.

4

Moving into a Leadership Role

When top performers are promoted into managerial roles and become responsible for other people for the first time, they experience two transitions simultaneously. Not only do they have to make the shift from individual contributor to manager but they must segue from follower (or individual contributor) to leader.

Like all passages, this one is challenging because new skills and values must be learned and old habits discarded. One danger here, though, is learning only part of what you need to know as a leader. You may acquire the critical managerial competency of delegating, for instance, but fail to develop a leadership vision. Or you may struggle to reconcile the managerial imperative of "getting things done" and the leadership mandate of developing people. In teaching and coaching senior executives, we've learned that most new leaders tend to emphasize those aspects of the role predicted by their personality. Detail-oriented people tend to focus on execution; big thinkers gravitate toward vision.

Moving into management is also a tricky passage because jumping from an individual to a team or group perspective requires a huge leap of faith. For the first time in your career, you're being asked to get work done through others rather than do things yourself. Some people find this shift tremendously disconcerting; it's what happens to some star athletes who retire to become coaches and can't understand why their players don't think and play the way

> One of the most significant development experiences in my career was my first supervisory position, where I was responsible for developing, evaluation, selecting people—something I couldn't get done sitting at my own desk. That to me was very significant in my own growth.
>
> BOB GLYNN, CHAIRMAN, CEO, AND PRESIDENT, PG&E CORPORATION

they did. Or it's similar to the experience of becoming a parent; your whole perspective shifts when you become responsible for someone else who needs your support and guidance.

Let's examine this passage in more detail and see how two new leaders dealt with it in different ways.

Challenges for First-Time Leaders

When you move from being an individual contributor to a manager, you must learn a wide range of new skills, including delegating, holding people accountable, developing direct reports, building a team, selecting people for positions, and so on. In terms of leadership, you must value the ability to get work done through others.

Rather than enumerate every value and skill that comes with this passage, let's consider the challenges people face as they deal with these new values and skills.

Challenge 1: Losing an Identity

Most newly anointed leaders begin their new job with great enthusiasm and energy, excited about the chance to lead rather than follow. Almost immediately, however, many neophyte leaders experience a sense of dislocation. Those who have a professional affiliation—accountants, engineers, technical experts, and others—find that they're being asked to give up or at least subordinate this identity. This is not easy to do, even with the intellectual awareness that it's the right thing to do.

People tend to want to cling to the identity that has made them successful. The technical person, for instance, has been immersed in the world of software, hardware, and systems, always thinking of himself or herself as a computer expert or technology guru. As a manager, however, the primary responsibility is people problems, not software problems. As much as the technical person might grasp the rationale for this transition, the reality is a shock to the system. She has to forge a new identity as a manager, and that can be difficult because she must give up her professional identity in the process. She may respond to the prospect of this identity loss some-where between two extremes—by micromanaging or, at the other extreme, completely abdicating responsibility. These reactions are a way of coping. When the manager looks over her direct reports' shoulders or ignores them completely, she doesn't have to take on a new managerial identity.

Challenge 2: Seeing Your Star Dim

The people who often have the most trouble with the predictable passage into leadership are the ones who were stars—the star sales-person, the tech genius, the brilliant numbers-cruncher. They were stars because of their individual contributions and, as managers and leaders, they can no longer rely exclusively on their individual tal-ents. Their challenge is to become willing and able to help others become stars. This can irritate people who relished being in the spotlight and receiving credit directly. In a very real way, this pas-sage challenges people about whether they want to be leaders. Do they want to give up a measure of personal glory in order to bring glory to the team?

Challenge 3: Balancing People and Tasks

This simple requirement of leadership can completely confuse new leaders. Sometimes new managers feel that leadership, in addition to being time consuming, requires the patience and wisdom of a Zen master to achieve the right balance between people and task.

In a managerial role, you need to focus on getting things done and motivating, developing, and communicating with people. In certain instances, getting things done may require you to push people very hard, to demand more than they believe they can deliver and ignore their needs for the moment. In other circumstances, you may have to allow your people room to fail and learn, sacrificing results for development, retention, or commitment. Because there's no magic formula for achieving this balance, first-time leaders often find themselves in a quandary about whether tasks or people come first in a given situation.

Let's look at how two executives we know dealt with these challenges in different ways.

The Rugged Individualist: Ron

Ron was a salesperson at a large pharmaceutical company who had done extremely well in his four years with the company. A former military officer, Ron was strong-willed, disciplined, independent-minded, and smart. He took to sales immediately, and his supervisor recognized his talent and gave him a great deal of autonomy. Ron spent most of his time in the field, calling on physicians and detailing products; he developed terrific relationships with doctors and hospitals that resulted in a tremendous number of sales for his division and personal rewards for himself.

Naturally, Ron wanted more than financial rewards for his work, and the company responded with a promotion to sales manager. From the moment Ron took the job, he hated it. He found himself bewildered when his salespeople didn't deal with situations in the field as he had. He had no insights into how to coach his team or give them useful feedback, and he felt as if he were wasting his time and energy when he had to conduct performance reviews or have discussions with people about "their priorities" rather than the priorities he had identified for them to address. Ron also felt uncomfortable in his managerial role. Just about every day when he was in the office, he came up with reasons to get out into the field. He missed the interaction with physicians and the recognition he received from others when he made a big sale or was sought after for advice on medical issues. Being a strong individualist, Ron didn't talk to anyone about his feelings. He never complained to his supervisor, and he convinced himself he should tough it out, figuring he'd grow into his new role, especially as so many around him believed that being an effective manager was the path to getting ahead.

He didn't grow into his role, and a little more than a year after his promotion, Ron was recruited to another pharmaceutical company as a senior salesperson. Ron couldn't face "going back" in his own company, and so he had to leave.

The Reformed Individualist: Denise

Like Ron, Denise was a star in Ron's company who was also promoted into a managerial role. Denise was a physician who had joined the pharmaceutical company with the hope of balancing her personal life with her role as a doctor. She was assigned to a research team, and because she did very well in moving a compound into early phase trials, she was promoted to manager.

We met Denise a few years after this promotion. We had been called in to coach various executives at her company, and we were reviewing the results of 360-degree feedback with them. We were struck by how uniformly positive Denise's feedback was.

All the members of her team noted that she was an excellent communicator and highly empathetic, and that she did a good job setting clear goals and objectives and holding people to them. When we discussed this feedback with Denise and told her how uniformly impressed we were with what we observed, she laughed and told us that we would not have been so impressed three years ago. She explained that her first 360-degree feedback results shocked her. Her people claimed that she was lacking in people skills and consumed by her focus on breakthrough research. When she was a researcher, she had worked long hours as a member of a research team, and as a new manager she expected her team to exhibit that same relentless drive on their projects. As a result, she did a poor job of meeting the "tasks versus people" challenge, communicated unreasonable expectations to her team, engendered frustration and even resistance among her direct reports, and was on her way to being terminated.

Fortunately, that initial 360-degree feedback alerted Denise that she wasn't handling her first leadership position effectively. She had a good, development-oriented supervisor who talked with her about the problems she was experiencing and followed up by assigning Denise an external coach. The coach helped Denise uncover some of her assumptions about leadership, and Denise thought long and hard about whether she was willing to change her approach or if she was better suited to be a researcher. Ultimately, she decided that she could have the most impact as a leader and made a successful effort to learn and grow in her new role. She learned to consciously adjust her expectations and motivational style to the unique needs of each person who worked for her. She committed herself to being an outstanding coach by practicing listening. She didn't lower her targets for her team, but she did become an excellent motivator of people.

How a Company Can Help First-Time Leaders

Some companies, such as Novartis and Bank of America, have put in place extensive programs and systems to support individual contributors as they make the transition into leadership positions. Other companies, such as Intel and Honeywell International, have put in place well-regarded "dual ladders," which allow technically oriented leaders to grow in prestige and promotions without climbing the managerial ranks. More companies are beginning to realize the importance of this transition, recognizing that their people will experience some degree of adversity in this passage and that it is front-line managers who translate the strategy, convey the culture, and select the most new employees. These organizations know that the adversity of a new leadership role can spur leadership learning and growth, and for this reason they try to increase the odds that this learning and growth takes place. Many companies have focused new-manager transition programs on the first one hundred days of the leadership assignment, combining assessment with feedback and coaching. The goal is to increase self-awareness, which is the essence of this passage, and to increase the possibility of success and learning as individuals adapt the mantle of leader.

Consider whether your company provides the following resources for people going through this passage:

• *Development of leadership skills.* This is probably the most common resource that companies make available, and it usually involves classroom teaching of skills such as delegation, communication, and the like. In our experience, the best leadership development programs blend learning methods, cognitive information, emotional experience, and self-confrontation. Some companies are providing Action Learning programs for new managers, in which participants learn while addressing a significant business issue.

• *Assessment or feedback process to determine how people are handling the first-time leader transition.* The company assesses and monitors the transition rather than assumes that because people have been selected for a leadership role, they'll be able to handle it. This process can be as simple as providing feedback to new leaders about how they're doing to having more formal programs involving coaches who discuss this feedback with new leaders and help them create plans to meet the learning goals that are part of this transition. Coaches can help new leaders think and talk about the values and skills they're struggling with as part of the passage.

• *Boss assistance or coaching.* It's been said that people learn how to be a boss from their own boss, and some companies take this axiom to heart; they encourage bosses to coach their people through this passage. In fact, more companies are even evaluating leaders on how well and how many new leaders they develop and enable to succeed. From formal mentoring programs to less formal one-on-one discussions, bosses can share their feelings and knowledge about what this particular passage entails. They can observe the new managers in action and provide continuous feedback about where they are struggling. This doesn't mean bosses should take on a protective persona and watch their direct reports' every move. They should, however, make themselves available to new leaders and provide assessment to those who need someone to help them when they're struggling to incorporate new values and skills into their work style.

Ideally, your organization is providing you with some or all of these resources. Even if that is not the case, however, you can take advantage of the learning in this passage.

The Normality of Struggle

Most people struggle with their first leadership position. In fact, if you make a seamless transition from individual contributor to manager—if you don't have any bad days, doubts, or fears about your leadership capacity—then you're probably in denial or your company culture prizes self-confidence so much that you find it difficult to acknowledge the challenge of this transition. Most new leaders experience some difficult moments in the first year or so in a new position. To deal effectively with them, do the following:

> I learned a lot from [my first boss]. He spent time with me—a lot of personal time with me because it was a small organization. He was teaching me the things that he had learned. He had built these businesses from nothing. It was an extraordinary thing—the value of a mentor who is older, more experienced, and has seen the battles, to take someone under their wing. This is a tremendous boost to their future.
>
> RAY VIAULT, VICE CHAIRMAN, GENERAL MILLS

• *Reflect and talk about the feedback you receive.* For many people, this is the first time they have received 360-degree feedback. In the majority of cases, this feedback challenges your self-perception. You think of yourself as tremendously empathic, and your people are telling you that you're oblivious to their concerns. Don't become defensive about what you hear and don't refuse to listen. Feedback is not a judgment of your capability. It is a summary of the perceptions of others. Force yourself to reflect on what you've been told and talk about it with someone you trust—your boss, a coach, or a mentor.

• *Heed your instincts.* This may seem like an odd bit of advice, but a great deal of business leadership is instinct—a fact that you may not learn in business school or as an individual contributor. Great leaders follow their gut when the data don't give them a clear choice, and many first-time leaders are overly reliant on analysis. In this first leadership job, you'll struggle with the dilemma of what you sense is true versus the expectations of your culture.

For instance, you feel the right thing to do is outsource a task, but the decision could result in workforce reduction. Or perhaps your company emphasizes keeping certain tasks in-house in order to exert control over processes. This is a dilemma, and much of leadership is managing dilemmas ("right versus right" choices) rather than solving problems. Dealing with dilemmas becomes easier with experience. Early in a leadership career, though, you have to remind yourself to try to satisfy expectations without doing so at the expense of what you believe. People fail during this passage because they ignore their instincts and try to please others. They try to meet their boss's expectations or conform to organizational norms and never form their own point of view. In fact, a key challenge of this passage is to both support your boss and differentiate yourself from your boss, sometimes at the same time. Those who try to satisfy their boss as repayment for their promotion to leadership may temporarily succeed because they meet expectations but ultimately fail as leaders because they've never developed their own take on things. Without this personal perspective, leaders can't create original, compelling visions; they come off as ungrounded or fickle.

• *Make the time to focus on people.* This goes back to the challenge of "tasks versus people." The reflex is usually to focus on tasks; you want to deliver great results to prove to everyone that you deserved your promotion. Fight this reflex. Be rigid with your schedule and priorities, making sure you create time for the dialogue and conversation that results in people development. Sometimes this expenditure of time may seem less efficient, but it is an essential element of leadership and supervision. Commit yourself to signing up for training, working with a coach, or just being conscious of people's needs and concerns, and devote time to people-related learning.

• *Grasp the network of influence and politics.* Some new managers take to this right away, but others resist it. The independent individual contributor may have always disdained what he feels is subservience to others and believes people should be judged based on their work alone. This idealistic perspective is fine in an ideal world, but the organizational world reflects society, and we haven't found many utopias. Networking is absolutely essential for leader-

---

I remember (early on when we were preparing the filing for Chapter 11) when I had the conversation with the team when we had been living here on Chinese food. It was every single night, and it was six days a week. We had a conversation about what we were needing to do. I said, "We are going to have to now start to behave like this might go on for ever." I still remember one of the guys in the group and the look on his face. I think he thought I meant that this *was* going to go on forever. I said, "This is going to go on for much longer than any of us can imagine, and we are going at sprint speed, and we can't do that forever. I want people to take weekends off; I want vacations to get scheduled. That doesn't mean that I'm not going to call you but you've got to get out of here." As I said, I had no idea how long this was going to take. We had to come up with a way to chunk out the work and bring it back to the team. We chunked it out to a couple of key guys here and had them constantly bring stuff back in. For a while, we met every day.

BOB GLYNN, CHAIRMAN, CEO, PRESIDENT, PG&E CORPORATION

---

ship. Understand power and where it comes from, how things get done in your organization, what tradeoffs are made, and who has influence. Build your own network so that you can gain support for your initiatives. This isn't about being a game-player; it's not about being sycophantic or manipulating people. Instead, it's about learning the network and how it functions and plugging yourself into it.

• *Don't abuse your power.* Maybe this won't be a problem for you, but in the name of speed or efficiency or "directness," some people who are promoted into managerial jobs suddenly become the worst type of boss. The power associated with advancement reinforces their arrogant tendencies, and they become directive, controlling, and always right; they make unnecessary demands, antagonize support staff, and generally engage in negative behavior. To avoid abusing your power, keep the learning matrix in mind. When you believe you have nothing to learn, you're being arrogant and vulnerable to these types of power abuses. If you approach the job believing you have a lot to learn, you'll be much less likely to apply your positional power crudely.

We've found that first-time leaders learn to use their power appropriately by *studying how other leaders they respect use their authority.* They see how these leaders navigate around roadblocks without being a bully and how they build coalitions rather than engage in melodramatic behavior. It's also useful to study leaders who abuse their power to understand what not to do.

• *Do the right thing, but don't be convinced you always know what the right thing is.* Again, this may sound like a Zen paradox, but the point is to have an open mind about what the right course of action is in a given situation. Some new leaders are so zealous about following their beliefs (the opposite of the politicians and those who focus only on results) that they offend everyone with their self-righteousness. It's great to do what you feel is right, but leaders need to recognize there are shades of gray when it comes to right and wrong. Until recently, the Bank of America had as a key value for leaders "do the right thing." Over time, however, it became clear

---

Just when our management group had achieved a major market victory, entitling us to well-earned bonuses, the then-chairman of the company intervened and said, "I'm going to make a big decision here." He canceled the bonus program, full company. He had made a wrong decision, which created our company's overall bad results, and even though my department—and a few others—had actually done a very good job and contributed strong numbers, he punished the whole company. That led me to realize this is not leadership. It is not the right way. You should take the blame, but you shouldn't punish the people who have produced the results. It was an unfortunate decision in my opinion. The net result of it was that within six months of that time, I left the company.

RAY VIAULT, VICE CHAIRMAN, GENERAL MILLS

---

that "the right thing" by one group of stakeholders might be exactly "the wrong thing" for another group. The bank has recently modified this key value to "make good decisions," which reflects the relative rather than absolute aspect of doing right.

Listen to other people's points of view, even if you initially find them off-putting, and be open to negotiation and compromise. This does not mean that you should always negotiate and compromise. Good leaders learn when and how to pick their battles. This is the passage where you start learning this lesson. Be conscious of how you look and sound to others when you start fighting for what you feel is right. Listen to yourself. Are you objectively weighing other ideas and opinions? Are you considering other options besides your own before digging in?

Early Learning for Future Payoffs

Some new leaders skate through this passage without doing any of the things suggested here. They intimidate others, they ignore their doubts and uncertainties, they act supremely self-confident, and they get great results and ignore people. If management isn't astute or paying much attention, it may look like these individuals are doing fine in their first leadership role and well on their way to one with greater responsibility. Eventually, though, what they haven't learned in this passage will be manifest in the motivational climate they create for others and, ultimately, in business performance.

Business publications have been full of stories recently of top executives who have failed miserably because they never learned how to communicate and empathize with their people or because they persisted in running their divisions or companies like micro-managing individual contributors rather than real leaders. Enron is probably the classic example of an arrogant culture in which incompetent leaders created an environment in which people either "got it" or were deemed stupid and candidates to be "ranked" and then "yanked" (terminated). As the Enron case demonstrates, arrogant leadership can look successful for a while, and companies still have senior executives in place who cannot motivate and lead others. These people probably never learned to value the leadership requirement of having a vision, getting work done through others, or learning to manage their own potential for derailment.

Our point is that what you learn in this early passage will pay off in the future. For instance, this is the first time that you'll have an opportunity to create a culture of your own (within your group) and lead change. These are two of the most difficult tasks a leader faces, and you probably won't master them in this passage. You can, however, learn a lot about the skills that will give you an advantage for mastering them later on. In fact, many first-time leaders fail at leading change the first time, but they reflect and talk about their failure and gain an understanding of what went wrong that serves them well in their next change-leadership assignment.

This second leadership passage, therefore, is where you create the foundation for the rest of your career as a leader. It is fine to make mistakes here, as long as you're conscious of what they are, why you went wrong, and how you might change what you do the next time.

5

Accepting the Stretch Assignment

All passages represent a test in the mythological sense of the word. In myths, the hero must reach down deep inside himself and determine if he has the inner resources necessary to slay the beast or complete the journey. The stretch assignment, perhaps more than the other passages, represents this type of test. Are you capable of moving from expert to learner as you encounter situations where you lack critical skills or where you have to shift your perspective?

As the name implies, a stretch involves moving outside your comfort zone. As in exercise, you feel the resistance when you're pushed beyond your normal range. Though people today often lobby for stretch assignments—the international posting is a particularly desirable one for ambitious executives—they may have a different reaction when their wish becomes reality. By definition, a stretch means you're doing something for which you lack the experience and expertise, and this can cause you to feel inadequate and angry.

There are many types of stretches, but they always involve moving to a new assignment where you lack the skill, knowledge, or attitude necessary to do the new job effectively. For instance, moving from a functional to a general manager job is always a stretch. For the first time, you must view the business holistically and break away from a singular, functional perspective. Even the smartest, most experienced functional head isn't fully prepared for this task, and that's why it's a stretch. (It's also why a business is most vulnerable when a new GM is appointed.) It's also a stretch when you skip a step in the logical managerial or career progression, jumping over others because of your unique skills or accomplishments.

A stretch can involve everything from a first international assignment to managing a significantly larger group of people to moving into an entirely new functional area. A stretch doesn't necessarily take place with every promotion or new job; you may only need to acquire a bit more knowledge or acquire an easily gained skill to be successful. "No pain, no gain" is the rule of both the gym and the business world for stretches. As we'll see, some people are better at dealing with this pain than others.

> For a period of almost eight years, I had a new job almost every year. Sometimes it was just a switch in responsibility; sometimes it was a change in function; sometimes it was about a change in the company. I think this high frequency of change and the need to face new uncertainties led me to where I could master special assignments. All of these assignments concentrated my thinking in doing something new, and ultimately being really stretched.
>
> THOMAS EBELING, CEO, NOVARTIS PHARMACEUTICALS

The Pain in Stretch Assignments

Stretch assignments are often humbling. Even if you actively lobby for a key job with the European office or are eager to obtain a general manager position, once you're there you're likely to be blindsided by what you don't know. The sheer magnitude of what you need to learn and the pressure to learn it quickly can create all sorts of counterproductive reactions. Let's look at one person who handled a stretch assignment poorly and one who handled it effectively.

Curtis: Dealing with Overconfidence

Curtis was brilliant at business development. He had thrived as the top business development person at one of the country's largest corporations. He had the perfect pedigree—a top-tier-school MBA, a great track record at a top consulting firm—and was a high-performing, high-potential individual with ten successful years at the corporation. It would be fair to say that Curtis had never failed in any significant way in his business career, and when he was appointed to head the major division of this corporation, he went into the job with arrogance bordering on hubris.

Although the assignment was a stretch for Curtis, he didn't see it that way. Curtis probably would not have viewed being elected president of the United States as a stretch. He was supremely confident and certain he possessed all the skills and knowledge he would ever need to handle any job. What he didn't have, though, was the ability to focus on the details, and his new job required this focus. It was the type of business that was highly regulated, and any company that wasn't vigilant about record keeping and statements made to analysts and the media could easily get in trouble. Curtis's company did indeed get into trouble within a year of his appointment, and it was due to his exclusively big-picture perspective. He was great at coming up with strategies for exploring and expanding markets and telling the company's story to analysts and the press, but he couldn't be bothered with the nitty-gritty details of budgets, financial reports, legal documents, and operational plans, and he wasn't interested in learning how to master these details, which were crucial to his position as a division head. After some time, his division was facing regulatory investigations and missing forecasts provided to corporate.

Amazingly, Curtis solved his problem by being appointed CEO of another company shortly thereafter that also required him to stretch in a similar way because, as CEO, the capacity to move back and forth between the big picture and operational details is a requisite for the role. Curtis told us he valued his big-picture style. He also seemed closed to learning or expanding his repertoire. In fact, he had built a logical case for why details were "other people's expertise." Not surprisingly, his new company also faced regulatory reviews and challenges, and Curtis was soon fired.

Charles: Managing a Short Attention Span and Volatility

Charles was named CEO of a major corporation before he turned forty. A superb consumer-marketing executive, Charles had a reputation for driving others the way he drove himself. Charles had been diagnosed with attention deficit disorder. He had a limited attention span and was also volatile—sometimes erupting in outbursts more suitable to a child than a business executive. His supervisor coached him in how to manage his derailers, but he was often left in position until he could prove his maturity while others around him were promoted. Despite these flaws, Charles delivered business results—growing revenue and profitability of his company. This ability prompted the board of a major public corporation to take a chance on Charles. This company, though, was different from any of the ones Charles had worked for or led in the past. Not only was it primarily a business-to-business organization but it produced highly technical products and services. When Charles's appointment was announced, many of his new company's employees questioned the selection.

From the start, Charles was stretched in a number of directions. It was his first time being the CEO of a public company. It was his first position with a business-to-business organization. It was the first company where the focus was on technical products. Fortunately, Charles did not attempt to impose his consumer-marketing approach on his new company. Despite his temper and attention span, he knew he had to monitor his impulses, and he didn't become angry or impatient about what he didn't know. Instead, he recognized he had a lot to learn if he was going to be successful, and he brought a fierce concentration to this learning. He spent part of each day absorbing all the technical knowledge he needed to grasp to be a leader of the business. He wasn't afraid to admit to his team that he didn't know something, and he relied on them to educate him about the business. Though Charles still drove himself and other people hard and pushed for results, he was open to adapting his approach. As a result, he's done extremely well as CEO and so has his organization.

Different People, Different Outcomes

Both Charles and Curtis had tremendous self-confidence going into their stretch assignments, and both had earned that self-confidence through their extraordinary effectiveness in previous positions. Both had a certain amount of arrogance and a temper; they both drove their people hard. How is it possible that two leaders who are similar in certain ways can react so differently to a stretch assignment? Why was Charles open to learning and Curtis wasn't?

One explanation might be that Curtis had never failed before, and Charles had experienced some failure; Charles had already discovered that he didn't know everything. It may also be that Charles came from a blue-collar background, whereas Curtis grew up with advantage. Charles had learned how to overcome setbacks and obstacles in his personal life; Curtis had not. Curtis, though, might have handled his stretch better if he had been prepared for what a stretch assignment entailed.

Common "Hurts" During a Stretch

On the plus side, stretch assignments are exciting. When you're working internationally, leading an integration or acquisition team, heading up a business unit, turning a company around, or managing a large number of people for the first time, you're going to be turned on by the challenge. It's a big assignment in a refreshingly new environment, and your success can mean a lot to your company and your career.

As exciting as these jobs are, the initial adrenaline rush subsides and you're left wondering whether you really can handle your new responsibilities. When you start making mistakes, realizing that you don't "get it" it hurts. The hurt comes in different forms, and if you are aware of what these forms are, you'll be better able to learn from them. When you realize that your response to this passage isn't unique to you—that hurting in different ways in a stretch assignment is normal and useful—then you are in a better position to tolerate it and learn critical new skills, knowledge, and values. Here are the three ways most people hurt during a stretch:

1. *Feeling like a victim.* "Why are they doing this to me?" is a common refrain when people suspect they're not qualified for the assignment they've been given. They're right, of course, but that's the whole point. You may be angry that your leadership didn't know you were going to have trouble with this job. As you're struggling to make informed decisions in areas where you don't have enough knowledge to make them, you may feel like the company should have prepared you better. The assignment may even feel like punishment. Some people beat up on themselves, furious at their perceived inadequacies.

Keep in mind that "they're doing this to me" may be true because corporate life is a test; if you complete the test successfully, you are more developed and thus able to handle more responsibility. The intent behind the assignment may be to obtain business results, as well as to develop you as a leader. They didn't give this assignment to someone else for a reason, whether or not that reason is apparent. You're the one who has been tabbed as an individual worth developing, and that's why you're the one struggling with the assignment. This may be cold comfort, but it should provide self-motivation to get through it by learning as much as possible.

2. *Perceiving skepticism or hostility from others.* Plum stretch assignments are coveted, and those who don't get them may react badly. These reactions run the gamut from coolness toward the

"stretchee" who was chosen to outright hostility. Others who weren't candidates for the job may also react negatively, feeling the stretch job should have been given to someone in their function or with a specific type of background. Whatever the situation, be prepared to encounter some unpleasant reactions from the new group of people with whom you'll be working. Other coworkers may also resent your appointment as head of an overseas business if you're not from that country or have no experience working there. Typically, this resentment lasts until you've demonstrated that you have something to contribute.

Overcoming the skepticism and hostility of coworkers is a great learning experience. Every leader encounters a dubious audience at different points in his career, and learning how to work effectively despite this reaction is a good skill to possess. In this passage, leaders learn to be patient with both themselves and others and allow their performance to speak for itself. Rather than being confrontational or discouraged by a less-than-warm reception, leaders discover that they can win most people over simply by doing a good job.

3. *Realizing you don't know what you need to know.* This really hurts. It's a shock to discover that you're unqualified in some way for a task or position you've been given. Imagine what happens when you move from a functional job to a GM position—a common stretch assignment. For the first time, you need to see the big picture, to break away from your functional perspective, to understand and appreciate all functions. If you're a marketing group head, you may realize you don't know enough about finance to do your job. Or you may be trying to solve a business problem and realize you've never had to think about all aspects of the business at once, and that's the only way to solve the problem.

The worst way to respond to not knowing is by pretending you do know. When people take on stretch positions, they sometimes respond with rigidity. Rather than try to increase their flexibility by expanding their capacity, they fall back on their old way of doing things. In a true stretch assignment, relying on old approaches rarely works. But even if it did, it would defeat the learning goal of this passage. When you admit you don't know, you take the first step toward increasing your capacity to adapt. You listen more intently, ask more questions, and test new behaviors and theories. Eventually, you find a new way to be effective. This adaptability serves leaders well, not just in this passage but in all subsequent passages in their career and life.

How to Handle the Stretch for Maximum Learning

Carol was recently named head of HR for a large company after successfully running a line business. She was known as a terrific developer of people, and so the CEO of the company, hoping to enhance the reputation of HR, decided that Carol was the perfect candidate for the top HR position, even though other HR professionals may have been more qualified, based on their broader HR experience. The CEO was aware that this assignment would be a stretch for Carol, but he also knew that development and talent acquisition were the two major issues facing the company; so he appointed Carol. We've been working with her to help make this transition go smoothly, and in one of our sessions together, Carol observed that she had learned three things about the assignment:

1. To trust her instincts because she didn't know enough to rely only on her experience
2. To assess whom she could and couldn't trust on her team
3. To determine how fast she should move to change things versus accept the status quo

Carol has the right idea. Her first point about trusting instincts is a leadership lesson we've emphasized earlier, but it's especially relevant here. In the midst of confusion and uncertainty because of your lack of knowledge and skills, trusting your gut is critical. This is a challenge for many executives who have always trusted their experience or the data. In a stretch assignment, you don't have this luxury. Relying on your instincts involves a certain amount of self-reflection rather than external analysis. You need to contemplate what *seems* like the right decision or course of action, even though you don't have hard evidence to back up this feeling. Remind yourself that your instincts have served you well in the past; you wouldn't be in a stretch assignment unless you had made some good intuitive choices. We're not suggesting that you should rely on your instincts for every decision, but use them when you simply have no other way of knowing what to do.

Her second point about team trust acknowledges that instinct will only take you so far; there are times when you must rely on experts who have greater experience and expertise in an area than you do. This means you have to interact with your team members— make the time to talk to them, listen to them, and get to know them—so you can figure out whom you can lean on when necessary. Certain people you won't be able to trust; in these instances, you must set limits. In many instances, we've seen a new appointee to a stretch position undermined by team members who are pursuing their own agendas; they're taking advantage of the team leader's vulnerability and waste valuable time on pet projects or even sabotage his efforts. If you can't trust people in your stretch assignment, monitor their activities closely and don't depend on them to deliver for you.

Carol's third learning is developing a sense of how quickly you can step in and start making changes. This is a complex issue, in that you don't know enough to be sure what changes are war-

> I discovered the advantage of not being an expert, in the sense that you can sometimes see the essence of problems and the position at hand in a new way. I had to learn to collate a sample of input when I could certainly not rely on one single expert. I would basically collect opinions, and I learned to formulate ideas this way to make decision making even better.
>
> THOMAS EBELING, CEO, NOVARTIS PHARMACEUTICALS

ranted, at least initially. The temptation when you don't know something is to rely on the status quo. Of course, if you just follow the footsteps of others or rely on past performance when you know change is necessary, you'll still fail. Here it helps if you have a network within the organization with whom you can discuss contemplated changes and the advisability of implementing now rather than later. Someone who knows the politics of the organization can help you assess the impact and can coach you through the difficult decisions that usually come with change. Carol is reaching out to as broad and diverse a set of advisers as possible, sometimes obtaining conflicting advice, which then helps her clarify her own instincts.

Finally, we would add one other approach for handling this passage effectively: *Be aware of where you are as a leader now, where you need to go, and how you might bridge this gap.*

A stretch assignment is a great opportunity to develop what you're missing. The very nature of a stretch is that you're going to be doing things you haven't done before. If you're conscious of the skills, knowledge, and values you're missing, you can focus on acquiring at least some of what you lack. If you don't know what your development needs are, then learning is a hit-or-miss endeavor. Your boss or a coach can help you become more aware of the gap.

How Organizations Can Help

Some companies are astute about stretch assignments. Kraft, for instance, has become known as the "cradle of CEOs," in part because they make a concerted effort to place their best people in jobs that stretch them just the right amount. Executives at Kraft often develop the flexibility, leadership instincts, and team management skills that are part of this passage, and as a result they make great CEO candidates. For years at GE, their Mobile Communications business served as a de facto leadership testing ground. By GE standards, it's a small ($1 billion) business, making it a good place for leaders to be thrown into jobs for which they're not fully prepared. We know at least two people who headed that business: John Trani,

CEO of Stanley Works, who went from Mobile Communications to become CEO of GE Medical, and James McNerney, who was in the running to be CEO of GE and is now chairman and CEO of 3M. For both of these strong leaders, the early stretch assignment of running a smaller business unit, taking a multifunctional perspective, growing revenue and profitability, balancing growth and execution, people and tasks—trained them for increasing responsibility and subsequent success.

Although not every organization has the resources of GE or Kraft, every company can maximize the learning potential of this stretch passage by doing the following:

• *Make sure a stretch assignment really causes an individual to stretch.* A challenging assignment for one person isn't so challenging for another. A job that merely requires someone to work harder and faster isn't necessarily a stretch. Nor is a task that demands a little more knowledge but not a lot. We counsel executives that in succession planning and in selecting leaders for new roles, they need to evaluate a stretch, based on the individual and her particular set of knowledge, skills, and values. They need to make these assignments based on their understanding of this person and how she needs to develop. For development, stretch requires moving into the unknown, and this requires a significant amount of trust on the part of the leader making the assignment. It goes without saying that too much stretch or an impossible goal is demotivating.

• *Provide tools and processes to help people with this transition.* Companies should take a cue from GE and create a type of "laboratory for learning" during the stretch assignment. They don't have to use a particular business as this laboratory, but they can use sophisticated training processes that have the same effect. Action Learning, for instance which we have written extensively about, is a process that gives a group of leaders a significant business challenge—a stretch assignment—but also incorporates learning tools and coaching. In this way, people can fail without significantly setting the organization back. To tackle the Action Learning assignment, they need to stretch, but they don't imperil a business if they make a blunder. Because the stretch involves a real problem or opportunity that faces their company and because management reviews their work on the assignment, they approach it with the same seriousness as they would a real task. (See *Action Learning: How the World's Top Companies Develop Their Leaders and Themselves* by David Dotlich and Jim Noel.)

• *Stretch your own thinking about whom to stretch.* Too often, companies limit stretch assignments to a certain group, such as early-career or high-potential leaders, believing that learning only takes place when individuals are relatively young or that people have the flexibility of youth. As a result, they miss chances to help more senior leaders learn and grow. In any given company, even highly talented leaders get stuck in ruts; they're doing the same things repeatedly and effectively. A stretch assignment can extricate them from their ruts and motivate them to get back on track to learn something new and different.

With an organization's support, stretch assignments provide the diversity of experience necessary for leadership growth. We've found through our research and coaching of successful people that most leaders cope well with the adversity that comes with a stretch, as long as they don't pretend to be unrealistically confident and thus inhibit their own ability to reflect or to stay conscious of their new learning.

6

Assuming Responsibility for a Business

Few passages in the life of a leader are as fulfilling as becoming a general manager. We've alluded to this passage in earlier chapters, because becoming the head of a business can be a stretch assignment, involve the risk of substantial failure, and occur when you join a new company—all at the same time. It is such a significant passage that we need to focus on not only its upside but the downside for leaders who are not open to learning.

It's fair to say that this is the passage that separates the future CEOs from the pretenders. For the latter, instead of being a pathway to higher leadership positions, this passage becomes a dead end. These people, seduced by power and deluded by arrogance, not only fail to achieve a more senior leadership position but squander the opportunity to run a business on their own. The job they thought was a dream becomes a nightmare.

Letting go of past beliefs and practices and opening yourself up to new ideas and approaches is important in all passages, but the nature of this transition makes letting go and opening up a particularly difficult challenge. When people are named to head a business, they feel like they've arrived; in most companies, these positions are highly coveted. It's very difficult to display humility when you feel "chosen," and many GMs, in our experience, succumb to arrogance. We often counsel senior executives that in their ascent to senior ranks, their jokes become funnier, their insights become brighter, and their viewpoint more intelligent—all due to the fact that no one wants to take them on. This can contribute to hubris, arrogance, and derailment. After a career-long climb to an apparent summit, you need to recognize that the peak is an illusion. If you persist in believing that you have been anointed rather than selected, your high perch will turn into a precipice, and sooner or later you'll fall off.

To translate this metaphorical warning into business language, let's look at what assuming responsibility for a business really means.

The Mind-Set of the Business Leader

When people are selected to run a business, it's the culmination of years of learning and sacrifice. In many instances, it's the fulfillment of a dream. Most executives have sacrificed time with their families, gone through periods when work was a seven-day-a-week proposition, and made some very tough decisions about jobs and people. When they're named general managers or division presidents, they've reached what many of them have thought of as a capstone position. As a business head, they have tremendous autonomy and authority. For the first time, they get to call the shots. Though they have a corporate boss, this individual generally gives them plenty of leeway. In certain instances, heads of businesses become community leaders. When these businesses are located in smaller towns or foreign countries, GMs may become local dignitaries—ambassadors representing all of General Motors, IBM, Ford, or the Bank of America. They're treated with tremendous respect (and sometimes subservience) by people in the community and invited to sit on local boards and participate in civic decision making.

We worked with a top executive with a large corporation who was appointed to a country manager position in China. As part of the appointment, he lived in a mansion, was called upon by diplomats, and attended fabulous parties. At the end of his successful tenure, he was transferred to a staff position in Milwaukee, where both he and his wife suffered significant re-entry shock. It wasn't the staff job that was a problem, but the loss of the prestige, perks, and autonomy of being a country head was hard to exchange for what they perceived as a boring life in an American city.

Although most leaders enjoy the GM position more than any they've ever had (and often more than any other they will have), there's a cost. Specifically, the profit-and-loss responsibility is a big change from their past positions, when they were primarily responsible for decision making that was removed from P&L tradeoffs. Just as significantly, they're moving from running a "partial" business as a functional leader to running one in its totality. As we've discussed, this means moving from a monofunctional to a multifunctional perspective. It means selecting people for their team, creating a culture, and being a ceremonial as well as a practical head of business. It also involves creating external as well as internal relationships. Functional managers generally aren't concerned with forging relationships with regulatory bodies, community groups, and other external entities.

Not only is there a great deal of knowledge and skill to acquire, but GMs must also acquire a distinctive mind-set. They need to value their people and their development much more than they did as functional managers. They must become accustomed to seeing more broadly and thinking bigger than they did within a singular function. They have to become comfortable dealing with a range of people, including a hostile reporter one minute and a competitive threat to the business a minute later. Perhaps even more challenging is the loneliness that some of our clients report. Some general managers are surprised to discover how truly alone they are for the first time in their business lives. Up until this point, they were part of a team. There was always someone to confide in and work with on an equal basis. As the cliché goes, "the buck stops here." They are singularly accountable for the business. They are the ones who are judged by the financial scorecard. Unlike their previous positions, they can't complain to or about their boss, at least not in the way they may have done in the past. Their boss is not a constant presence but rather a distant observer, representing a very different way of managing upwards.

GMs are jugglers, and this is probably the first sustained juggling act they've ever performed in public. Earlier in their careers, they could focus on specific tasks and goals. Even if they did different things, their responsibilities were limited by their jobs. A business head, however, is responsible for everything. This is a psychological shift leaders need to make. They must accept that they're going to be jumping from one area to the next, and they won't have time for everything. It's magical the way good GMs keep all the balls moving, but it's also a bit overwhelming to think about sustaining such a performance.

Finally, most GMs enter their jobs assuming they've been well prepared for their new responsibilities. Certainly, they've been prepared in one sense of the term. Most MBA programs review the requirements and tasks of the GM, and they provide students with a good concept of the skills the job requires.

A functional manager position, too, provides people with experience in different areas that may be useful when they run a business, but in coaching and teaching hundreds of GMs, we have come to believe that leading a functional area may not be a particularly good training ground for the GM position. Though most companies

> First of all, be yourself. Be attentive. Don't shirk on your career. Care for your consumers. Care for your company. I've seen so many people being obsessed about their own career that they have forgotten how to make the difficult decisions. To really get diversity of experiences you have to rotate into different functions, different countries, corporate operating units. Only then can they compliment themselves on their strong leadership.
>
> THOMAS EBELING, CEO,
> NOVARTIS PHARMACEUTICAL

route their best people from functional roles to heads of business, this isn't ideal preparation for the passage.

Our colleague, Ram Charan, has suggested that the best way to prepare someone for being a business head is to give him "little" GM jobs, such as letting someone run a smaller business, as in our example of how GE used smaller businesses to minimize the risk in training future GMs. Charan has also noted that running small but complex, interdependent businesses such as a teenager's lawn-mowing business (marketing, payroll, revenue generation are all required) may be the best early training for a future GM. Excellent GMs learn to make tradeoffs, and this requires focusing on multiple priorities simultaneously, continually shifting attention and em-phasis, and making decisions with a full view of how one decision might affect other alternatives.

The Dangers of Being a Know-It-All GM

In coaching and counseling CEOs, we have noted and written about the fact that the need to appear confident, combined with the lack of good feedback available to senior people, can lead to arrogance and egotism. As a new GM encounters situations for which he has no experience and no clear course of action (which is what new GMs mostly encounter), arrogance becomes a shield to ward off the fear that he's not up to the task. To help guard against this attitude, be aware of the following common dangers in this passage:

• *Disdain for the functions.* People tend to go into the GM job with biases against functions in which they've never worked. They refer to financial people as bean counters, or they talk about how HR professionals don't understand business issues, or they believe that marketing people are all sizzle and no steak. As a result, they don't learn to use all the functions in a way that will make them—and their business—successful. They become over-reliant on the functions with which they are comfortable or once worked in, even if those functions should not be driving the business. Because they're so certain that their function is critical for business success, they never can view other functions objectively.

• *Myopic focus on performance and results.* Obviously, performance and business results are important, and it's understandable that when you are given P&L responsibility for the first time, you are naturally eager to deliver profits and avoid losses. The financial scorecard for a business, unlike a functional budget or objectives, is displayed for everyone to see, and it makes GMs acutely and consistently aware of their results. In large corporations, it is not unusual for divisional presidents or GMs to eye each other's results and engage in overt competition about who is more successful and therefore more deserving of promotion.

But GMs must also learn that hard results need to be balanced with "softer" responsibilities such as developing people and shaping a culture. In the long run, these responsibilities affect the bottom line as much as, if not more than, creating a strategy and driving toward objectives. Business heads must recognize that they can only sustain strong performance and results by juggling multiple priorities. In certain instances, they need to make tradeoffs, sacrificing some of their time and the business's money to communicate with people or to develop the next generation of leadership. They may never have had to make these tradeoffs before. Now in their new role, they have to learn how to make them in real time.

• *Failure to challenge the business model.* This is a particularly challenging issue for business heads who take over from a strong leader to whom they owe their promotion. They feel beholden to carry on the strategy and traditions of their mentor or former boss. It feels disloyal to deviate significantly from the norms that have been established. Yet challenging the business model is something all GMs must do regularly. This is a passage in which leaders have to establish their own point of view, to create their own theory of the case. In the past, they may have simply adopted the point of view of their boss, but this is unacceptable behavior for a GM.

Learning to question an inherited strategy or system is tremendously difficult for some new business heads, especially if surrounded by alumni who helped the previous GM create that strategy or devise the systems. But it's absolutely essential at this leadership level and for all levels above this one.

The Role of Paradox in Business

The leaders who get the most out of this passage—the ones who not only excel as business heads but go on to become outstanding CEOs—adopt values and embrace a perspective that can seem antithetical to this position, at least at first glance. Valuing the unfamiliar, displaying a hang-in-there mentality, and accepting paradox may not be the first things that come to mind when you think of a business head, but these traits are exactly what helps these leaders learn and grow. Let's look at each trait and why it is so important:

• *Value the unfamiliar.* In teaching many GM programs, we counsel GMs that it is easy to become lulled at the top of an organization by the role and the perquisites that accompany it. Many new GMs have difficulty holding a balance between confidently challenging the system to change and staying humble and in a learning mode at the same time. Within the first six months on the job, you'll discover that your knowledge and skills, no matter how great, are inadequate for the requirements of the job. The best GMs learn how to build great teams because they need great teams. It takes a group of diverse experts to run a business; no one person can possibly know enough. Rather than be intimidated by people who know more than you in a given area, recruit these people and empower them. They're the ones who will save you. As long as you value their superior knowledge rather than feel threatened by it, you'll be able to cope with tasks for which you aren't prepared. Be aware that it often takes time and conscious effort to value the unfamiliar. Take time to reflect on whether you're valuing it. Are you shutting people out from your team who know more than you do? Are you responding angrily when a savvy direct report suggests another way of doing things that goes against your traditional approach? Do you find yourself asking members of your team not to "show you up" in team meetings, when all they're really doing is pointing out issues you couldn't possibly know about?

• *Display a hang-in-there mentality.* This is something different from either a conquering or defeatist mentality. The former mind-set creates unreal expectations; you're not prepared to learn from the setbacks and obstacles that are part of the job. The latter mind-set is a common reaction to these setbacks and obstacles. When the job proves overwhelming and the decisions impossible, some people get down on themselves and shift into defeatist mode. "Hanging in" means having the courage to deal with the ambiguity and uncertainty of the job, even though it's scary at times. It means having patience and trusting your instincts, even though the short-term results aren't what you'd hoped for.

We're working with a top executive who is in the process of taking over a business from a highly successful general manager. Tim has been an enormously effective "product" person with this company; he is skilled at developing products and dealing with the financial side of the business, but he doesn't have much experience with cultural or people issues. Initially, these issues have frustrated him. Tim is accustomed to having a boss to turn to when facing a major problem, and now he has no one. The ambiguity surrounding some of the people decisions he's facing—who to select for his team, how to deal with "solid citizens" who have made a major contribution to the business but are not high-performers—is especially difficult for him to handle. He is struggling with the inherent conflicts of potential decisions. If he terminates the good performer in order to upgrade his team, how does he mitigate the impact on the motivated culture he wants to establish? Tim told us he never realized that he would be grappling with so many difficult questions without easy answers.

There is no magic solution for Tim except to display the fortitude to get through this rough passage and the energy to keep working hard, despite the difficulties he encounters. He also needs to develop his own theory of how the business should be run, believe in that theory, and use it, along with his instincts, to make decisions.

• *Accept the paradoxical nature of work.* Paradoxes occur with increasing frequency at every managerial level, but they're especially acute when you run a business. A paradox is a situation in which a decision is required and two equally appealing alternatives with equally negative factors present themselves. Common paradoxes in running a business include "short term versus long term," "centralization versus decentralization," "standardization versus innovation"; most cannot be solved, only managed, and GMs must learn to behave paradoxically. For example, business heads need to move fast and have patience. In other managerial jobs, moving fast generally takes priority over patience. Here, though, people need to be aware of the implications of their actions. For instance, as Tim is learning, there are times when it's unwise to act on the impulse to fire someone because of how that action will affect the entire organization; a business head's actions are magnified by the position, and even though getting rid of someone may be the right thing to do in one sense, it's the wrong thing to do from an organizational perspective. Learning when to move fast and when to have patience, therefore, is a skill all business heads need to master.

Finally, there's the paradox of values and results. As we've discussed, P&L responsibility drives GMs to focus on results, but they need to learn to balance values with this drive. One of the most difficult decisions a GM has to make is sacrificing short-term gains in order to maintain a cultural belief or norm. For instance, a business experiences pricing pressure and begins to lose margin and profitability. The GM has to decide where to rein in costs. One alternative is increasing employee co-pay on health costs. For example, the business may have paid 80 percent of the costs for employees and emphasizes this as a perk—part of the "great place to work" atmosphere in which it takes great pride. The business head knows that passing more of the cost of health care on to employees is the right thing to do from one perspective—it will help avert downsizing—but that it violates a cultural tenet.

Learning to function effectively amidst these types of paradoxes is crucial, and this is the passage where this learning should take hold. Too many business heads, however, feel more comfortable solving problems than managing paradoxes. They like to see problems crossed off their "to do" list. They prefer black-and-white choices—always opting for results over values, always moving fast, and always acting with confidence. Here and on higher leadership levels, the best executives find a way to manage paradox, making decisions situationally and reflectively rather than uniformly and reactively. And in so doing, they reinforce an authenticity in their leadership style that will serve them well.

Promotion as Passage

It helps to view your promotion to GM as a passage rather than an end-point. A passage connotes movement and growth. If you see being a business head as a static experience, you'll be shocked by what occurs. Typically, most GMs reach a point of being overwhelmed and paralyzed, usually in the third, fourth, or fifth month on the job. During the first two months, they are usually able to convince themselves that it's only a matter of time before they get on top of things. Then it hits them. They're never going to get on top of things! A lot of self-doubt can enter at this point, and they may even question whether they've got what it takes to be a business head.

Some people are simply not cut out to be a GM, and it is hard to face this reality if you live in a corporation in which this position is valued above all others. If you feel in your gut that this is the wrong spot for you—that you prefer staff work to P&L responsibility, for example—then you must face into this reality courageously. We have coached several GMs who could only admit privately that they didn't enjoy the role. This may be difficult to do in the short term; it's tough to be named a business head and then admit you're not up to it. But in the long run, you and your career will benefit.

Fortunately, most people who become GMs have self-selected for the job. Extensive succession-planning processes and vetting usually ensures that the right people are selected, and typical GM candidates are tough-minded, smart, energetic, and highly motivated.

These traits will serve you well when you feel you're managing too many issues or have too much to learn in too short a time. As we've emphasized, what helps people get through a passage successfully is an openness to new ideas and approaches. Admittedly, this particular passage requires you to absorb a huge amount of new information and to acquire skills you may have disdained in the past. The good news is that if you've made it to a business head level, you probably have the capacity to apply yourself effectively to all this learning. This passage may be a trial by fire, but you're in a better position than most to withstand the heat.

7

Dealing with Significant Failure for Which You Are Responsible

The following paradox is at the heart of this passage: *If you've never failed as a leader, you'll never be very successful.* The best, most accomplished CEOs almost always have at least one significant failure on their résumé. The CEOs who fail spectacularly—who place wrong strategic bets, invest in growth channels that don't develop, mislead analysts and investors—are often leaders who have never failed before. As Richard Branson, chairman of Virgin Atlantic has said, "The best developer of a leader is failure."

Some executives are adept at avoiding this passage. They only take jobs for which they're qualified and avoid risks in whatever jobs they hold. They "manage upward" well and are able to advance because of their competence. They can advance only so far, however, before their lack of resiliency, adaptability, and perseverance—all traits acquired in this passage—precludes them for higher-level leadership positions. Eventually, they find themselves in situations where they make serious errors of judgment because of their failure-free background. If you'll recall our earlier matrix in Chapter One outlining the importance of adversity and diversity in both career and life, these are the individuals who don't value diversity of experience.

> If you want to increase your success rate, double your failure rate.
>
> THOMAS WATSON SR.

Other executives take risks and experience significant failure, but they aren't open to the learning it holds. They've gone through this passage with their minds closed and don't benefit from its lessons. They deny their own responsibility for the failure, blaming everyone else and never thinking about what they might learn from their mistakes. Invariably, they will make the same mistakes again.

There are also very smart, skilled leaders who allow failure to define them. Rather than being open to the learning of this passage, they close themselves off because they are devastated by their mistakes. They are convinced that their careers are ruined and that they lack the stuff of which true leaders are made. Instead of seeing their failure as a result of a given set of circumstances, they personalize it and see themselves as failures.

As a passage, significant failure can be complex, prompting a number of counterproductive actions. To help you turn this passage into a leadership development experience, you need to unravel this complexity and see failure for what it really is.

Perception Versus the Reality of Failure

Significant failures can take many forms. Perhaps the most common one is failing to meet major organizational expectations. For instance, you're assigned responsibility to develop a new product line, and you fail to deliver the prototype product by the deadline. Or perhaps the product design is flawed, rejected by focus groups, or simply can't be priced at the right margin level. Or you may be responsible for a product introduction that fails, or you're a business head who presides over three consecutive quarters of declining sales. A boss, a board, or the shareholders deem you accountable for the problem, and your punishment can be anything from not receiving a promotion to being fired. These situations happen frequently in companies everywhere, but to the leader to whom it is happening, it often seems as though he or she is the first and only person to have the experience.

A major failure can also be self-perceived. In other words, your boss or some other external party doesn't perceive that you are not delivering, but you feel this as a fact yourself, acutely. Your team may have encountered significant competitive pressure, or endured the introduction of a disruptive technology by new market entrants, or just had some bad luck. And even though no one blames you for this failure, you blame yourself; you feel that others were depending on you, and you let them down. You may also feel you've failed to achieve a career goal, and you are furious with yourself for not doing what was necessary to achieve at the level you have set for yourself. Perhaps you are one of those leaders who is a perfectionist and will therefore, in your own eyes, never be good enough, never achieve enough, never be successful enough.

It's also important to consider what you did that caused a failure. If you seek the diversity of experience that's crucial for leadership, you naturally are going to find yourself in situations where you don't have all the knowledge and skills necessary to do a job effectively. Therefore, you may cause a failure because of what you don't know. This doesn't excuse the failure, but it does provide insight

---

I'm not sure that I've slowed down to think about what I've learned [from the experience of leading a company into and out of Chapter 11 protection]. What I knew from the leader part of it was I really had to have the mind and the heart and the confidence of each key member of my team. I had to find a way to connect with them personally and also to lead them as a group. That was where I spent my time. It became clear to me long before the Chapter 11 happened that this was going to require a team that was really willing to aim at an objective outcome. We had a meeting. I needed each person to sound off. Folks didn't hold back their reservations and ideas and concerns. Those meetings were the best ones.

BOB GLYNN, CHAIRMAN, CEO, AND PRESIDENT, PG&E CORPORATION

---

into what you can learn from it. Or you might fail because you vio-
lated organizational values, treated people poorly, or were guilty of
a breach of ethics. At GE, as in most companies today, people who
fail for business reasons are given a second chance. Individuals who
fail because of a values violation are not.

Although your actions may produce a significant failure, this
isn't always the case. You may simply be the victim of bad luck; you
happened to take over a business right when the economic downturn hit or your team or division experienced production delays,
computer glitches, pricing pressures, or any number of challenges.
Significant failure may also be caused by internal politics, by a competitor, or by any number of other outside forces.

No matter what form failure takes, however, it humbles and embarrasses us all. Public humiliation, whether it involves being fired, being chastised by a superior (or not being chastised when you feel you should be), or being grilled by the media, ridiculed by columnists, subjected to comments in on-line employee chat rooms, forced to answer questions about your poor quarter in front of your peers—these situations are not fun. Private humiliation—feeling as if you let yourself and others down—is equally tough to take. The good news is that if you're open to understanding why you failed and able to acquire new knowledge and skills from it, you'll grow as a leader.

> I felt that I had been dealt a set of cards that were going to be very tough to play. I sure wasn't going to leave the table. I had an obligation to lead the business back to a successful outcome. I owed this to the share-holders. I knew I needed to play these cards the best possible way you can play them.
>
> BOB GLYNN

John Reed of Citibank, for instance, became a better leader
after his company was in trouble and he brought it back from the
brink than he was earlier, when he presided over a thriving
Citibank. Steve Jobs was forced to depart Apple, only to become a

stronger leader and years later return to take over the company. Edgar Bronfmann lost a significant portion of his family's fortune in selling their holdings in Du Pont (which doubled in market cap) so he could invest in Vivendi, which didn't, only to resurrect himself as a current leader in the music industry. Significant failure deepens leaders, giving them the resolve and resilience they might not have had when they were running successful ventures.

Given the complexity of failure, it's easy to do the wrong thing. Let's look at how leaders most commonly err when faced with major breakdowns and losses.

Three Don'ts in Dealing with Failure

Humiliation and embarrassment hamper our capacity to learn. It should not be a surprise, therefore, that many leaders don't think straight or learn much after they've made mistakes or suffered setbacks. In fact, they typically react in one of the following ways, and we'd like to alert you to what they are and how to avoid them:

1. *Don't let failure define you as a person.* We've seen highly talented, fast-track leaders derailed by a single failure. In many instances, this happens when people internalize failure rather than separate the event from who they are. Even if you made a stupid mistake, you aren't stupid. Recognize that anyone who works long enough will experience a significant failure at least once in his career. The worst thing you can do is dwell on the failure, running it through your mind again and again, second-guessing yourself and beating yourself up for whatever mistake you made (or think you made). After acknowledging the failure and accepting responsibility, you need to let go of it and move on. Put your mistake in perspective—this is a natural, predictable part of any career—and refuse to allow it to dominate how you lead.

In the past few years, we have worked with a number of former partners of the failed accounting firm Arthur Andersen. The vast majority of global partners played no role in the firm's demise and were only witnesses and not participants in the collapse of a great company with which so many were identified and committed. However, the range of reactions on the part of senior leaders demonstrated the importance of perspective. Those with the ability to separate their role in Andersen from their identity as a successful and competent professional were able to quickly move on to other opportunities and become successful again. Unfortunately, others personalized the experience for no good reason and became stranded, literally and figuratively, in their careers.

2. *Don't seek scapegoats*. Realistically and naturally, most leaders who fail in a big way react defensively. Corporations may give lip service to failure being a good learning experience but, in most instances, corporations treat failure brutally. There is so much pressure on organizations for performance that relatively few companies can forgive or forget failure easily. At the same time, if you respond defensively you're likely to waste this teachable moment. If you blame your team or anyone else for the setback, you're not likely to examine your role in the failure. You may convince yourself that you had nothing to do with the problem when, in fact, you helped cause it. And even if you bore no direct responsibility for the failure, blaming others discourages self-examination and the acceptance of responsibility—two critical leadership traits. Resist this blaming reflex and instead absorb the blame. This doesn't mean saying *mea culpa* for everything that occurred under your leadership. You don't want to further deepen your predicament by dwelling on all the things you did wrong. There are gracious ways of accepting responsibility for failure. You can admit what you did wrong, explain the context for the mistake, and make a commitment not to let it happen again; you can demonstrate that you've learned a lesson that you will apply in future situations.

3. *Don't limit your thinking to the event itself*. Yes, it's important to learn from what went wrong and act differently if the same circumstances present themselves in the future. Significant failure,

however, is an opportunity for internal, as well as external, learning. Ask yourself what it says about you as a leader that you did X instead of Y. Consider how your approach or values may have caused you to contribute to the failure. In many ways, it's easier to look at failure from an external perspective; you can define exactly what you should know or do in the future. An internal perspective is more difficult. It relates to who you are, not only as a leader but as a person. Did your arrogance contribute to the failure? Was your mercurial nature a contributing cause?

Four Dos in Dealing with Failure

In the emotional upheaval surrounding significant failure, it helps to have specific things to do in order to learn and grow from the experience. We worked with one CEO—let's call him Joe—who failed in a highly public and spectacular manner. He promised results that he did not deliver. The media focused on him extensively and dissected his leadership, decisions, and style; his board finally fired him. Joe, however, was a bright, talented leader. He had gone through many of the passages, learned from them, and matured as a leader. There was no reason to suspect that he wouldn't do well as CEO, except for the fact that he had never really failed in a major way.

Although Joe was understandably upset by the public nature of his ouster, he resolved to get back in the game. Before doing so, he carefully analyzed, thought about, and discussed what had gone wrong. He hired a personal coach to help him deal with the issues that the whole episode had raised, including his overconfidence (which the media claimed had hurt the company on a number of fronts). It took a while, but Joe is now the CEO of a midsize software company that is performing well, and his rebound from failure was due, in part, to the regimen he followed in the wake of his dismissal.

When you fail, you should also consider taking the following four steps:

Step 1. *Examine your decisions that catalyzed the failure.* More specifically, look at your attitudes, as well as your actions, that may have caused a loss, poor result, or negative outcome. Even if an attitude or action wasn't the main cause, consider how it may have influenced the outcome of events. Ask yourself why you decided what you decided. Were you afraid of taking a risk? Were you taking too much of one? Were you too stubborn and didn't listen to your team's advice? Which of your personality derailers (see *Why CEOs Fail*, by David Dotlich and Peter Cairo) may have occurred under stress and contributed to your failure?

Step 2. *Talk to your boss, a coach, or some other trusted adviser about this incident.* Many people cannot discuss their failures. Some leaders have come to believe that "failure is not an option" and "discussing failure is not an option either." This type of swagger is not leadership; it is denial. Discussing how things went wrong is painful, and it requires courage to expose your vulnerabilities. It's even more painful because you're talking to someone you respect and trust; you don't want that person to think less of you. These conversations are important, though, because they allow you to obtain feedback, examine your assumptions, test your hypotheses, and come to terms with yourself and your role in failing. It can be useful to reflect on your failure by yourself, but you also need the benefit of an outside perspective. It's not so much that other people will give you practical advice about how to avoid this failure in the future (though that might occur) but that they can offer you insight about who you are as a

> Following a career setback, I had very clear goals in the short, medium, and long term that I was working toward, and I really simplified my life to focus on achieving those goals. There were goals in my personal life, my family life, my economic life, and my business. I literally sat down with a piece of paper and worked through all of that and decided this is the way I'm going to lead my life and this is what's important; this is what's not important. It was like a second birth almost.
>
> RAY VIAULT, VICE CHAIRMAN, GENERAL MILLS

leader and how you need to develop. They may note that your arro-gance or indecisiveness contributed to the failure or that you are rely-ing too heavily on your technical insights and not developing your emotional intelligence. Leaders often take these conversations to heart. They're motivated by their failure and open to learning about themselves as leaders, perhaps for the first time in years. Especially for highly successful people, failure offers teachable moments because it's such a surprising experience. Conversations with wise mentors and coaches help people capitalize on these teachable moments.

Step 3. *Reflect on what you might do differently in the future.* After you've analyzed why you did what you did and talked about it, the next step is to reflect on how you might respond in a more effective way when facing a similar situation in the future. Again, don't just think in business or strategic terms. Consider what you've learned from this particular failure that will serve you well in other positions and when you are faced with other decisions. Realistically, you may never again find yourself in exactly the same situation in which you experienced significant failure. You will, however, find yourself in many situations where the learning from this failure will come in handy.

For instance, many top executives who go through this passage have been overly controlling. Typically, they were under intense pressure and were convinced that if they worked hard enough and relied on their expertise, they could pull their team or business through a difficult challenge. Just as typically, they discover, on reflection, that this was the mistake that caused or contributed to the failure. They realize that if they're going to grow as leaders, they need to trust their teams, be honest with them, and ask for their help. No doubt they will encounter different types of problems in the future when a team-based solution is critical, and they will have the maturity to include their team rather than shoulder the entire burden of decision making themselves.

To help you reflect on what you've learned from your failure, ask yourself the following questions:

If you encountered exactly the same failure-related situation in the future, what would you do differently?

To do something differently, what would have to change inside you? Would you have to adopt new values, become more flexible, change your traditional approach in some way?

What did you learn about yourself from the failure? Did you discover that you were stubbornly set in your ways or too obsessed with results, or that you had to spend more time and energy developing people rather than businesses?

Step 4. *Summon the energy to persevere.* Failure is enervating, but the leaders who move forward are the ones who manage to summon the energy necessary to keep at it. Failure leaves you feeling defeated, but great leaders obtain the psychological resiliency that comes with this passage. There's no secret to acquiring this resiliency. It's simply a matter of digging deep inside yourself and deciding you're not going to be defeated, at least not in the long term. Focus on the job that needs to be done, the specific tasks that you're best qualified to accomplish. Discipline your thinking to avoid dwelling on your mistakes or the mistakes of others. Instead, force yourself to go after new goals with the same drive and determination you displayed before the failure. If this sounds like we're suggesting that you give yourself a pep talk, you're right. Great leaders have tremendous self-motivation and are adept at re-energizing themselves after they've been knocked down. What you'll learn from this passage is that if you summon this energy, you'll persist long enough to receive another opportunity to prove yourself.

Effects of Company Attitudes on Failure

How leaders deal with significant failure depends to a great extent on the company culture and industry in which they lead. Until relatively recently, some industries had done so well for so long that failure was an anomaly; there was a certain arrogance among companies in these industries, a sense that failure was what happened in other organizations. As a result, any leadership failure was dealt with in the harshest way possible, and people were so terrified of messing up that they did everything they could to avoid taking risks. Companies at the top of a business cycle, such as Internet companies in the late nineties, can also disdain failure and not be prepared for it when it arrives.

Though few companies have emerged unscathed from the economic downturn of the last few years, some still harbor an arrogance toward and intolerance of failure. Not only is this attitude unrealistic but it discourages leaders from learning a single thing from failure except to deny, deny, and deny some more.

Companies like GE that have enlightened attitudes, however, give people second chances if their failures were business-related (rather than values-related) and encourage the reflection and dialogue that creates a learning environment. At GE, people who had failed in major ways were invited to speak at their Crotonville training facility and tell present and future leaders that there was indeed life after failure. Although no organization can survive by treating mistakes and setbacks with unlimited forgiveness, it can increase the odds of thriving by recognizing failure as a natural part of the leadership life cycle. Essentially, the best attitude is when companies communicate something along the lines of the following: "You made a major mistake, but we believe you still have a great future as a leader. Prove us right by taking the time and making the effort to learn from what went wrong. And don't make the same mistake again."

Organizations often bemoan that some of their most talented leaders are stuck in their ways and unwilling or unable to change, even though they've been encouraged to do so. Despite coaching, training, and outright threats, they refuse to change their leadership style or adjust their attitudes. It seems nothing will motivate them to change—until they fail. This shakes up even the most confident people and forces them to examine all their assumptions and practices. In many instances, significant failure is a once-in-a-lifetime opportunity to change and grow as a leader, and companies should create an environment in which people are encouraged to take advantage of this opportunity.

8

Coping with a Bad Boss and Competitive Peers

Most leaders expect to work in consistent, rational environments, and most of the time their expectations are met. More specifically, they expect the people they work with to operate in certain ways: conform to cultural norms and practices, adhere to commonly accepted values, communicate honestly and accurately, and act like professionals. They also naturally assume that they'll behave like decent human beings.

When these expectations aren't met, even great leaders struggle to cope. Think about a boss you disliked or a coworker you wanted to avoid or ignore. Perhaps your boss was volatile, or maybe your coworker was overtly friendly but covertly withholding key information from you. The odds are that their behavior struck you as irrational. It's likely that you felt, at some point, that they had betrayed your trust, and you found it difficult to work with them afterward. They may have become the reason you left your company to seek employment elsewhere.

We consider this experience a passage, because most leaders will go through it at least once in their careers. Good leaders learn to use the passage to improve their leadership ability. Ineffective leaders let their anger and self-pity overwhelm them, and they don't take the time to reflect or talk about this emotional experience in terms that go beyond their immediate, visceral reaction. Good leaders resolve to understand the dynamics inherent in the situation and how their behavior may have contributed to creating it.

There's more to having a bad boss or aggravating coworker than meets the eye, and we need to understand that "bad" means different things to different people.

A Continuum of Badness

Making distinctions about "badness" helps us deal with it in its many forms. Rather than have a uniform reaction to every bad boss or peer, we can identify the degree of badness an individual possesses and thus create an appropriate strategy that will maximize the learning and minimize the trauma associated with this individual. The following "continuum of badness" will facilitate this process:

Annoying	Flawed	Value-Averse	Unethical

On the far left side of this continuum are people who annoy and irritate us. One may be a disorganized, noncommunicative, or distracted boss; another may be a temperamental, overly talkative coworker who exhibits behaviors that you occasionally find annoying. In most cases, these people have positive qualities as well, but their one negative behavior stands out for you and causes you to perceive them as bad. In reality, it's one *behavior* that you perceive as bad.

To the right of Annoying is Flawed. This is not just a particular behavior or attitude that's problematic but an ingrained aspect of their personality that colors their management and work style. This may be arrogance, perfectionism, volatility, or any number of off-putting qualities, but these traits are part of their persona and make them difficult to deal with at times. You consider them bad because you're intimidated by a volatile boss or find it unpleasant to work with a melodramatic coworker. We've written a lot about leadership derailers in other books, and we coach leaders to understand their derailment factors, which are career derailers for these individuals; good leaders learn how to work effectively with people who have these derailers—and know how to manage the derailers in themselves.

Value-Averse individuals are bad, not just because of a behavioral or personality factor but because they hold values that are in significant conflict with yours or those of the culture in which you both work. A Value-Averse boss, for instance, will constantly focus on "task over people" (or the opposite), ignore the importance of family or outside support, seek to undermine the boss, humiliate direct reports in public, act rudely to coworkers, or ignore the practices and beliefs the company stands for. Working for someone like this is challenging for many reasons, not the least of which is that you feel devalued as a person because something that is important to you is being undermined by someone in authority. Although you might trust someone who is Annoying and retain some trust in a Flawed individual, it is difficult to trust a person who is Value-Averse.

The Unethical boss or peer is bad to the extreme. This is someone who may cavalierly violate established ethical principles, laws, and regulations, or may lie, cheat, and manipulate as if he were above the laws that govern human behavior. Working for or with people like this is hell. Not only can't you talk to them about their behaviors but you feel guilty collaborating with them on a project or supporting their success in any way.

The farther to the right bosses or peers are on the continuum, the more difficult they are to work with. Nonetheless, each type has a leadership lesson to offer those willing to learn.

Besides the continuum, you should also consider the consistency factor. It's much easier to work for and with individuals whose behavior is predictable. If, for instance, your boss is irritating in the same way all the time, he's not as difficult as someone who irritates you in unpredictably different ways.

One leader we observed—we'll call him Tim—was a terrific boss in many respects, but he had wild mood swings. You'd go out to dinner with him one night and he would be charming, open, and friendly, but the next day he'd be cold and distant. There was no logic to his mood swings, at least none that his direct reports could discern, so it was very difficult to predict him and, ultimately, trust him. His direct reports felt that no matter how hard they worked or how great their contributions, Tim didn't respond appropriately. In fact, they might even fail to deliver or perform poorly, and Tim would sometimes respond with understanding, even kindness. Other times, when he was under stress but their results were good, he would be furious. To help people gauge Tim's changing moods, his secretary used to surreptitiously signal thumbs-up or thumbs-down so direct reports knew whether it was a good time to talk to him or avoid him. Tim's team learned to manage Tim— establishing control mechanisms and adaptive solutions so they could get work done, which is not uncommon in companies with multiple personalities and styles.

Bad bosses and peers can take on many guises, and they're not always the expected ones. For instance, the stereotypical bad boss is controlling, aggressive, domineering, or even bullying. But in reality, most bosses aren't bad in this sense, especially in large, professional, knowledge-based organizations where overt bullying behavior is generally not tolerated. Just because your boss isn't a bully, however, doesn't mean he's not bad in some other sense of the term. Consider the following three examples of leaders we have encountered.

Mark: A Risk-Averse CEO

Mark is an ineffective CEO of a medium-size public company, a man so exacting and deliberate that he lived and breathed financial reports and data and was generally uninterested in strategy, people, and organization. Although he was good at establishing metrics and measuring progress, his lack of interest in people gradually created an environment in which people were unmotivated, and over a two-year period, some of the high-performers left the company because of his unwillingness to take risks, focus on careers, or address the requirements of the future. His erosive leadership was only evident over time, and eventually he was simply unable to deliver on the financials he measured so precisely.

Marcia: An Erratic Boss

Marcia was a bad boss in a very different way from Mark. Marcia was a charismatic GM who initially attracted the best and the brightest to her team and then alienated them with her mischievous ways. Marcia was creative, extroverted, energetic, and playful, but she viewed established rules and procedures as "suggestions"—that were open to violation when circumstances required. She delighted in being disingenuous, circumventing rules, changing established goals and objectives, and holding meetings that included or excluded key people, depending on how she perceived a situation. She didn't mind if people were kept anticipating her next move, and her direct reports were frustrated and even angry at times, although they enjoyed Marcia's company and appreciated her creativity.

Robert: A Vindictive Boss

Robert was a good boss who became a bad boss because of a specific situation. A long-tenured CFO in his early sixties, Robert found himself being subtly marginalized and pushed aside by a newly hired CEO who didn't want to engender an age-discrimination suit from Robert. Instead, he brazenly recruited a CFO heir apparent and asked Robert to "show him the ropes." Robert became angry and resentful. Furious at his organization, feeling betrayed because of his long service, foiling his hopes to engineer his retirement at his own pace, Robert unconsciously chose to undermine his successor by giving him trivial tasks, withholding information, and preventing him from participating in key financial reviews. Though Robert was outwardly polite to his new direct report, he was privately vindictive, and his resentment leached into his overall leadership of his function.

Bad Peers

Peers, too, are bad in different ways. The stereotype of a competitive peer who will do anything to get your job or scheme to make you look bad in the eyes of the organization is more the stuff of melodramatic fiction, sitcom television, or movies than the reality of professional companies and firms today. Bad peers are typically bad because a boss has orchestrated a situation where competition between two or more people for resources, assignments, or promotions is fierce. Peers can be bad in confusing ways—one day they may be supportive and the next become competitive and withholding. Today's allies may suddenly turn into future competitors because of shifting organizational structures, priorities, or roles.

The point of all this is to consider bad bosses and peers in relative terms and consider them situationally. Don't jump to conclusions and assume someone is bad because his personality irritates you or you're angry at one particular action. It's possible that your boss is evil incarnate and that you should quit immediately, but this is rarely the case (although we coach many senior leaders who hold exactly this viewpoint). By keeping an open mind about how bad your boss or peer really is and in what particular way, you give yourself a greater chance to learn critical leadership lessons in this passage.

Questions to Ask Before Fighting or Fleeing

When you have a bad boss, your reactions may swing between an impulse to confront him or to look for another job. If you have a bad peer, you may have a similar impulse; you might not look for another job in response, but you may decide to avoid him or challenge him. (In coaching executives, we are no longer surprised to learn how focus on a boss or peer who violates expectations can turn into an obsession that is brought home, discussed continuously, or becomes the basis for an entire coaching intervention.) These responses, however, fail to take into consideration the lesson of the previous sections; bad bosses and peers vary considerably and change frequently. If you approach them with learning in mind, you'll tailor your approach to the particular individual and situation. Therefore, answer the following questions before taking action:

Where does your boss or peer fall on the bad continuum? Use the criteria we've provided to determine approximately where he or she resides.

Are you aware of the context for your boss's or peer's bad behavior? In other words, is he under an unusual amount of pressure or facing a difficult situation in his personal life? It may be that your boss has just experienced a personal loss or that his own boss is placing tremendous pressure on him. His bad mood may be an anomaly or the result of temporary stress. A few discrete inquiries can tell you if off-putting behavior represents who this person is or who this person is in a given situation.

Are you expecting too much? It's not unusual for people to look at bosses as mentors or even father or mother figures and coworkers as confidantes or sometimes siblings. When these individuals don't live up to their expected roles, people view them as bad. In fact, some bosses aren't particularly paternal or particularly adept as developers of talent. Similarly, some of us view our peers as friends and confide in them. Because we work closely with them and get along so well with them, we assume that they'll support us as a friend would and watch our backs when we're in trouble. Although coworkers certainly can be our friends, in certain instances they're not. They have their own agendas and concerns, and when our needs conflict with these agendas, they may not be particularly friendly or supportive. That's the byproduct of a competitive workplace. We deem these peers bad but, in fact, our expectations for them have been unrealistically high.

When you answer these questions, you'll have a much better sense of the way you should go through this passage. If, for instance, you find that you're expecting too much of a boss or a peer, you may find it easier to hang in there and wait until the pressure eases up and they return to their normal behaviors. In this way, you won't prematurely leave a boss who has much to teach you or cut off a potentially productive, collaborative relationship. Just as significant, you'll learn how to work with people when they're not at their best and tolerate a certain degree of bad behavior without making snap judgments based on this behavior.

Similarly, recognizing where someone is on the continuum and placing his or her actions in context gives you more information with which to make an informed decision. If you have an Unethical or Value-Averse boss, the right course of action may be to leave the company, and this is a good lesson for any leader to learn. However, if someone is on the continuum's cusp—somewhere between Flawed and Value-Averse—you may want to give him the benefit of the doubt and wait and see what happens. The choices you make in these situations will affect what you learn from this passage, so let's look at what you should be learning.

How Bad Bosses and Peers Help Create Good Leaders

There's more learning to this passage than may be readily apparent. In the heat of the moment, it may seem as if there's absolutely nothing to learn from bosses or peers whom you dismiss as jerks. In fast-paced companies, leaders typically jump to "the bottom line" about someone else. Their behavior is so obstructive to what you are committed to accomplishing that you believe the organization should deal with them immediately. They do something so aggravating and make your life so difficult that you're convinced they have nothing to teach you. Although they may not be able to teach you directly, indirectly they provide experiences that will serve you well in other leadership positions. Specifically, here's what you can learn from this passage:

• *How to motivate yourself.* Up until this point, your motivation has largely been extrinsic. Your boss or team has set goals that you've achieved. You've worked hard to please your boss or for the good of the team. A bad boss takes away this motivation. The very notion of making him look good through your creativity, productivity, or diligence seems impossible to accept. Nonetheless, you have to push through this negativity and work hard for yourself rather than for anyone else. The best leaders derive an intrinsic satisfaction from a job well done. They possess an inner drive to achieve and excel. This is your chance to develop this drive. The higher up leaders go on the organization chart, the more they must discover inner motivation rather than depend on someone else to motivate them.

Similarly, people need to learn how to motivate themselves to work with peers they find unsettling. Executives who nurture petty feuds with fellow employees end up squandering vast amounts of energy through in-fighting and sometimes jeopardize their business as a result. Famous feuds at the senior levels of business, such as those that have embroiled Disney and Pixar, Hewlett-Packard, Daimler Chrysler, and many others, are often personal in origin but costly and extensive in their impact. More significantly, executives who regularly feud with others find it difficult if not impossible to motivate themselves to work hard with a bad peer to achieve a common goal and sometimes resort to boardroom brawls, legal fights, or other tactics as a matter of course. Great leaders, however, motivate themselves to work well, even with people they find distasteful, in order to achieve common objectives. They have long ago learned the important lesson that peers and colleagues come in a variety of forms—some to their liking, others not—but that personal preferences cannot obstruct business goals and objectives. Great political leaders are often able to forge alliances with other leaders whose politics and values they disdain but circumstances require it. When a feud erupts, or worse, finds it way into the boss's office, boardroom, or media, nobody wins.

• *How to work in a system where you aren't protected.* When you have a good boss, you're protected to a certain extent. By protected, we mean that your boss can provide you with information, resources, advice from the next level, and insight when you really need them. Good bosses will intervene if you're having problems with someone else in the company, advise you on resistance and potential reactions from others, and generally keep you out of harm's way. This is fortunate, but it can also prevent you from learning how to operate without a protector. As a result, your dependence on your boss may prevent you from learning how to resolve difficult situations on your own or forming your own, independent network without your boss. In fact, we have seen good leaders struggle when a strong boss leaves the scene—because the boss has not only served as mentor but as protector.

With bad bosses, however, we have often seen the opposite. Leaders are forced to figure out how to plug into the organization. If you have problems, you have to solve them by yourself. Learning, sometimes the hard way, how a company really works, including alliances, resource allocation, political networks, and unspoken rules, is tremendously valuable. CEOs and other senior executives are inherently vulnerable; no one protects them or intervenes on their behalf. To be effective, they must be able to work the system. Being politically savvy and having strong networking skills are essential, and people acquire these skills when they have a bad boss.

• *How not to be a boss or a peer.* A negative example is a great teacher. If you ask a veteran executive to recall some of the memorable people he's worked with, he will sometimes name more bad bosses or peers than good ones. When we ask senior leaders to identify a critical development experience in their career as a leader, they often cite a bad boss who taught them what they didn't want to become as a leader.

These individuals have a tremendous impact on people's work lives, and over time this impact is often more instructive than destructive. This passage helps leaders become aware of their boss's derailers, which makes them more conscious of their own potentially fatal flaws. It's very difficult to perceive how your own arrogance or overly cautious behavior is hurting your performance as a leader unless you observe this negative impact in others, preferably in your own boss. Forewarned is forearmed; you've seen how your boss's derailer hurt his career, and you're not about to make the same mistake. A bad boss or peer is a reverse role model—one you can use to guide yourself away from counterproductive actions and attitudes.

> I was getting a lot of coaching from people who were different kinds of leaders than I was. I felt it was negative coaching. I felt it was coaching as a way to force me into the Honeywell image rather than coaching to help me become a better leader as the person I was.
>
> BILL GEORGE, FORMER CHAIRMAN AND CEO, MEDTRONIC

To take advantage of these three learnings, we recommend the following steps:

Step 1: *Choose an interpersonal strategy to manage the relationship.* If you work with continuous hostility toward your bad boss or peer, you're not going to learn much of anything. Therefore, you should choose a strategy that helps you cope with a difficult situation. Doing nothing is certainly one option, but we'd like to offer some other alternatives:

> Ask yourself, "*Why has this particular teacher appeared on my career path at this moment?* Viewing your relationship with a negative person as a teachable moment rather than something to be endured or overcome will open

you to new possibilities of managing the situation, including changing both your reactions and your responses. "What can I learn here?" can replace "How can I get rid of this person?"

Talk to your boss or peer about the problems you're having. Consult the continuum before opting for this approach. If your boss is on the far right side of the continuum, talking isn't going to do much good. If, however, he is on the left side and is a relatively reasonable individual, then it may be worth having a heart-to-heart conversation. It's difficult to level with a boss whom you find annoying, but it may be worth the discomfort if an honest conversation reduces the annoyance level.

Confront your boss or peer. In other words, push back. Rather than just talk, communicate that you can't accept the way he's treating you and that things need to change. This approach is more risky than just talking, but sometimes people need to see that you're angry or upset before they will be willing to consider changing their behavior.

Go over your boss's head. Tell your boss's boss about the problems you've having, and ask him to intervene. This action may escalate the tension between yourself and a bad boss to unacceptable levels, and you may even be fired. Remember, organizations are not particularly responsive to complaints about bad bosses. They tend to back the boss rather than the direct report. Still, it may be a risk you need to take to deal with an intolerable situation.

Quitting is also an option, but it's not always the best one. If you have great market value, and your family situation (or lack thereof) allows you to quit and find another position, this may be the right thing to do, especially if you have an unethical boss. We find that the situation often repeats itself, and some people are surprised to find their new organization filled with the same proportion of negative players as before, often because they have taken their own existing frame of reference along with them.

Step 2: *Ask yourself what your reaction to a boss or peer says about you.* Too often, people focus on all the bad things that a boss or peer has done to them rather than consider why this boss or peer has evoked such a strong reaction in them. Certainly, there are times when the problem is completely external to you—an underhanded, cruel boss is underhanded and cruel to everyone. Most of the time, though, people's perceptions of badness vary, and it is often due to the chemistry of a particular relationship. A volatile boss may seriously affect a direct report who is unaccustomed to volatility, whereas another can easily adapt to changing moods. You may have a lot of problems with a hypercompetitive peer, whereas someone else may have no problems with his intense desire to win, or even perceive it. Taking time to reflect on your reaction to a bad boss or peer and talk with a business coach about your reaction can help you learn a lot about yourself.

Specifically, ask yourself the following questions:

Does this individual remind you of someone from your past?

Does this person remind you of something in yourself that you don't like?

It may be that there's a particular type of person you have trouble working with. If you have higher leadership aspirations, you can't afford this blind spot. Or rather, you need to be aware of it and manage it. Think about why you can't stand arrogant people (perhaps because you have tendencies in that direction yourself) or why indecisive bosses make you crazy (perhaps because you're an impatient person). Your strong, negative reaction to a boss or peer may tell you something about your own weakness as a leader.

Step 3: *Define your values.* It's possible that you can't stand your boss or coworker because they do things that violate your values and beliefs. They may cut corners to get projects done fast or treat direct reports poorly. Whatever it is, use their actions as a catalyst for determining what you really believe in. Great leaders have strong beliefs, and this is a chance to think about and solidify the principles to which you adhere.

Why Reaction Is What Counts

People typically feel sorry for themselves when they have bad bosses, because they feel deprived and let down by their organization, or they suffer at the hands of an authority figure. They react angrily when they have competitive peers because they feel threatened, challenged, or vulnerable. Some may suffer loudly; others suffer in silence, but their dominant reaction is emotional pain. This reaction doesn't facilitate learning. As we've noted about other passages, it's not the event itself that harms careers but people's reactions to the event. You can choose to be miserable, or you can choose to make the best of a difficult situation.

Making the best of it means viewing your bad boss or peer as a teacher on your path rather than as an obstacle. Really bad bosses, for instance, can teach you a lot about trust. It's a terrible feeling when you think your boss has broken this bond of trust. If you're paying attention (rather than focusing exclusively on self-pity), then you're much less likely to commit the same error when you're the boss.

9

Losing Your Job or Being Passed Over for Promotion

This isn't about losing just any job or being passed over for a position that wasn't of much interest to you. Instead, it's about being laid off or fired from a company to which you dedicated twenty years of your life. Or it's about not receiving a promotion you had targeted for some time—an opportunity that rarely comes around. In other words, this passage involves a huge career disappointment—one that shakes you to your core. Although it was once unusual, this passage is increasingly common as companies restructure, reorganize, or seek to reduce employment costs.

Psychologically and emotionally, this passage taxes your resolve and resilience. It's extraordinarily difficult for many successful leaders to get their minds around the fact that they lost out to another candidate or that they were let go; it is ego-deflating and challenges their sense of self. Similarly, this passage can create tremendous anger, bitterness, and betrayal, and these feelings can stop leadership growth in its tracks. We are often called in to coach senior leaders in the middle of this passage, because the organization wants to "save them." We know from intense conversation this passage is difficult and sometimes emotionally wrenching.

Like the other passages, though, this particular adversity does help you become a more effective leader in a unique way. If you make the right choices and avoid extreme negative emotions, you can emerge from the passage as a more viable candidate for a leadership position than you were in the past. Just ask James McNerney (chairman and CEO of 3M), Bill George (former chairman and CEO of Medtronic), Jeffrey Katzenberg (partner in DreamWorks SKG), Jamie Dimon (chairman and CEO of Bank-One), Steve Jobs (chairman and CEO of Apple), and many other successful leaders who endured the pain of this passage, only to go on to another senior leadership role stronger and more insightful as a result. The key, though, is to view the adverse circumstances with perspective and insight.

Reaction Versus Reflection

To help you gain this perspective and insight, let's look at two leaders we have encountered in a senior leadership program who have recently entered this passage.

Aaron Reacts

Aaron was a senior executive with one of the country's largest corporations. He had worked for this company for more than twenty years, and he'd done well, receiving a series of promotions that helped him become the head of a function. When a GM retired and there was an opening, Aaron immediately told his boss he wanted the job. Like many executives, Aaron had thought a lot about running a business, and this was his opportunity. He lobbied hard to obtain the GM position, and the CEO told him he was definitely a candidate. His coworkers assured him it was a cinch; no one in the organization was as qualified for the job or had worked so long and so well for the company. Aaron was sure he would be rewarded for his loyalty.

He wasn't. The job went to an outside candidate. Aaron was at first humiliated, then outraged. He felt betrayed. He didn't know how he could show his face at work with any confidence, since everyone knew that he'd been passed over by the organization. Aaron felt strongly, "This is the end of my career, at least in this company! How can I expect my direct reports to respect me after something like this!" Nonetheless, he showed up at work after the announcement and immediately encountered the Chairman and CEO in the elevator. Unable to contain his rage, he confronted the CEO and indirectly accused him of being misleading. He also said he felt it might be difficult to trust the company or its leadership again. The CEO said he understood and exited the elevator when it stopped. An inherently melodramatic leader, Aaron then told the company's HR head that he was considering filing an age discrimination lawsuit because the person selected for the job was seven years younger than he. He continued in his negative mindset in working for his new boss and, not surprisingly, was eventually terminated, suffering two losses as a result.

Karen Reflects

Karen was also passed over for a promotion. Though she hadn't worked at her company for as long as Aaron, she too had her heart set on a promotion—a manager-of-managers position. More than that, her boss had promised it to her, assuming that she would reach a series of goals, which she in fact did. In her mind, Karen saw this as an opportunity to "separate myself from the managerial pack." For three years, she had been traveling at least two days a week to achieve one of the goals her boss had established—improving customer relationships. Not only had she traveled extensively and put in long hours but she had told her coworkers and friends that she was going to receive this promotion.

One day, Karen's boss called her into her office and broke the bad news: in a succession-planning review, one of the key, influential senior people in the company had problems with Karen getting the position; a confrontation several months before between the two of them had disappointed him, and he was blocking her promotion. Karen's boss told her she was embarrassed by the senior executive's political interference but that, for now, the decision could not be reversed. She reiterated that she felt Karen was doing a great job and that she would do everything in her power to promote her when another opportunity presented itself.

At first, Karen was as angry as Aaron. Unlike Aaron, however, she didn't allow her anger to shape her reactions to her boss. During that initial conversation, she had a negative impulse to lash out reactively but was able to overcome it. Nodding her head instead, she admitted quietly that she was disappointed. Still, she was tempted to quit. Karen felt that her boss didn't fight hard enough for her, and she wasn't sure if she wanted to work in a company where a top executive could roadblock her career because of one incident. For a few weeks, Karen struggled with the decision. She thought a lot about it and talked several times with a former supervisor who had recently retired from the company. Her mentor, who knew Karen's boss well, assured her that her boss meant what she said, that she was as honest as she was politically astute, that she would work to get Karen the promotion she deserved, as long as it didn't compromise her politically. Their discussions helped Karen recognize that one reason she didn't receive the promotion was her political naiveté. For years, Karen had disdained office politics and had never made an effort to form relationships with senior executives. If she had, her mentor said, she might have been able to overcome the resistance of the executive who prevented her from getting the position.

Though Karen remained angry about being passed over, the anger gradually diminished, and she realized her greatest opportunity to obtain the promotion she desired was to stay with the company and culture she knew well, at least for another year. During this time, she decided to work hard at being more of a networker to establish greater support among senior executives and to channel her achievement drive into improving her relationship with the executive who blocked her promotion. Rather than avoid him, she sought opportunities to interact with him, including serving together on an HR project team. It took two years, but when a subsequent opening occurred, she was promoted to a manager-of-managers job in another division.

Aaron reacted; Karen reflected. Despite appearances to the contrary, business runs on emotion, and skilled leaders learn to channel their emotions productively, no matter how daunting the task. Under the threat of being passed over, stalled, or blocked, high achievers often want to take immediate action to affect the situation, and that action is often negative. If you're passed over or lose your job, your immediate response will be negative. You're likely to beat someone else up or beat yourself up. In either case, you're not in a mood to absorb the learning this passage contains. At worst, your anger will get you fired or cause you to burn bridges. At best, your ego will be deflated, and you will make more difficult the continual challenge of leadership—to develop self-confidence and astute observations about situations and people.

Conversely, the reflection and conversation we recommend in all the passages will prove particularly useful here. This passage has ended more than one promising career we know of, for no reason other than an inability to manage emotions and impulses. Some people never recover from being fired or being passed over, even if they eventually do secure other jobs and promotions. Psychologically, they remain mired in the anger, bitterness, and self-flagellation that is common to this passage. We regularly encounter executives who are fueled by hostile urges developed years ago in their treatment by another executive or company. Therefore, take the time to analyze the adverse event that took place and articulate your feelings and concerns about it. We'll look at different ways that you can do so, but first we need to understand the dangerous points of this passage and how they destroy careers.

Signs of Self-Destruction

People enter this passage having failed before, but this failure is different in the sense that what takes place here is often psychologically devastating. A sea change occurs in the way ambitious people view their companies when they're passed over for a key promotion or let go. For years, they represented and championed the company, its people, and its values. Overnight, they believe they have become the object of the company's scorn, or at least its indifference. Just as significantly, being passed over or let go is beyond their control. With some failures, they may have contributed to their own demise, but it's someone else who decides they should be terminated or not get the job; the decision often feels as capricious and uncontrollable as fate.

In short, this passage, particularly at senior levels, can be especially disconcerting. It's more likely to challenge you if you have any of the following traits or are in any of the following situations:

• *Your job is the essence of your identity.* To some extent, who you are is defined by what you do. Problems surface in this passage, however, when your primary self-definition revolves around work, which is not unusual given the time demands and psychic rewards senior executives experience. When your friends are all related to your business activities, your leisure time is absorbed by networking or business transactions, and the social activities in which you participate involve people in your company or industry or carry a business agenda, your identity has narrowed significantly. As a result, you're emotionally vulnerable to any downturn in your career. Being passed over or fired is the ultimate downturn, and it's difficult to recover from this setback, let alone learn anything from it. There are communities in the United States (the affluent Connecticut suburbs within driving distance of New York City come to mind) where many senior corporate executives live. They work in related fields, they socialize together, and they may even vacation together. Thus when one of these people is fired or passed over for a promotion, he experiences a double setback. He feels like he can't show up at the golf course or go out to dinner without people observing and pitying him.

• *Excessive self-confidence.* Leaders need sizable egos or they wouldn't be able to exert an impact on large companies or business units; relatively few selfless people make it to the top of competitive corporations. At the same time, some people have healthy egos and others have unhealthy ones. The latter group views any criticism or defeat as a personal affront. For them, it's never "just business." Being fired or passed over is the ultimate personal insult, and some leaders can plunge into minor depression afterward or respond with great vindictiveness and fury. In either case, the learning is more difficult to obtain.

• *Long tenure with one company.* The longer you've been with an organization, the more difficult it is psychologically to deal with being terminated or passed over unless you have worked to prepare yourself. After an extended period of time, some leaders continue to believe in the rapidly disappearing psychological contract of years ago: that their company owes them for their years of service and that their loyalty will be reciprocated. This is rarely the case today in a performance-based, competitive marketplace. Some companies work hard to foster the illusion that employees are family, and only the most dire economic circumstances would create conditions for termination. But future economic conditions and company response are increasingly unpredictable. You may have even witnessed these events happening to coworkers but rationalized why they took place. When it happens to you, though, it's shocking. It seems unfair and even cruel for a company not to retain you or promote you, or to go outside for new talent when your only fault has been loyalty and long service. In these circumstances, you're highly vulnerable to feelings of bitterness and vindictiveness that can stymie your leadership growth. We have coached many executives through this passage, and the goal is to "let go."

• *Performance issues are cited as the cause of the action.* If you're terminated or passed over for nonperformance reasons, it's much easier to make it through this passage without enormous emotional upset. If you're part of a large downsizing triggered by an economic downturn or don't receive a promotion because a new leader has hired former associates, and the political nature of "people" decisions are obvious, you are less likely to become stuck in an anger stage. However, when you're told you haven't performed up to expectations, the criticism strikes at the heart of who you are and what you do. You can't justify or rationalize the action the company has taken, and so you're likely to respond with rage against the company or yourself. In either instance, you're making it more difficult to learn in this passage.

How to Grow from Being Diminished

Whether you're let go or don't receive the promotion you've hoped for, you can take a number of steps to make sure this is a productive passage in your professional life. First and foremost, recognize that this passage, like all the others, happens to the vast majority of leaders if they work long enough; in fact, it generally happens more than once. Beyond this general recognition, do the following:

• *Refuse to allow the event to define you.* We've offered this advice about the "significant failure" and "bad boss" passages, but it's especially relevant here. When we coach leaders who have been fired, we emphasize to them that they are more than the sum of their work roles and responsibilities. They are community leaders, parents, spouses, marathon runners, sailors, siblings, children, grandparents, and many other identities. Keep a sense of perspective about all aspects of yourself, refusing to globalize and "catastrophize" a single negative event.

• *Understand why it happened.* What you learn from this experience depends on the effort you put into grasping the learning the experience provides. You need to be brutally frank with yourself, which is something that senior leaders are discouraged from doing. If you made a significant mistake that directly caused you to be fired or overlooked, admit this mistake and probe the missing ingredients: Is the skill set at your executive level shifting or growing? Is this experience part of a pattern in your career—failure to execute, inability to think strategically, unwillingness to build a team, or some other common executive misstep? Do you recognize the conditions? Be aware that you may be in denial about a given event or blaming others; don't settle for the easy explanation. Ask yourself and others what really transpired to cause you to be fired or ignored for a key position. Work hard to gather the right data, and then analyze them rigorously. It is painful, but it is what great leaders do in this passage.

• *Use your support network.* This passage is particularly brutal, and going through it alone makes it worse. Tremendous anxiety surrounds being let go or passed over, and it requires "processing" or conversation to come to terms with events. Professional coaches, career counselors, and colleagues may be able to help you discern the causes and potential positive outcomes of this adverse event. Their empathy, advice, and confrontation will serve you well in the difficult moments when you'll be tempted to act out. As much as you may want to quit after being passed over or to rage against the unfairness of the company or leadership, or worse, become cynical and silently vindictive, you have to get yourself into a less reactive posture before making any career decision. The right support network and professional coaching can prevent you from making a decision you'll regret.

• *Develop a "what next" strategy.* One of the things leaders learn in this passage is that resiliency involves both attitude and action. Therefore, moving beyond an analysis of what you might have done or what you might do requires creating a plan based on an analysis of your options. If you were passed over, how does the new boss really look? Can he grow you or teach you? Is there another position in the company that you might have a chance of obtaining? Is it really best if you start looking elsewhere?

Sometimes, being passed over or fired is a wakeup call, and the action required needs to be significant. If you were fired, what do you need to do to get and keep another significant leadership role? Will your derailment potential follow you? That is, are you knowingly or unknowingly carrying personality factors that impede your effectiveness under stress? What type of company or job will provide you with the type of meaningful work you've been searching for and dovetail with your talents and interests? Create a plan and take action to avoid becoming stuck in a no-growth leadership stage. In working with leaders, we find that this "teachable mo-ment," even though it's painful, yields tremendous leadership devel-opment experience, increasing empathy, self-insight, and forward momentum when well managed. Most leaders who move through this passage cite it as key to their later effectiveness. "It called the question" or "It made me confront myself" are leadership growth moments that cannot be replicated in any leadership development program.

Finally, take your time. Action-oriented executives are often so desperate to take action after losing a job or being passed over that they take the wrong action—wrong, not just in the sense of ending up with a bad or boring new job but because it cuts short the period of reflection and contemplation that leads to real growth. Our stan-dard advice to high-performing leaders caught in this passage is "take your time, if you can." Many fully engaged, hard-working ex-ecutives long for a sabbatical or opportunity to reflect and regroup. When it comes, because they have chosen it or because of excessive anxiety, they want to end it and get back to work. A leadership career is a series of assignments and events, and the period between them, if available, is not only precious but vital for self-renewal. When you accept the first job that comes along and immediately plunge into the time and energy demands of the new role, you de-prive yourself of an opportunity to take stock of yourself. It takes a powerful event to force you to contemplate who you are as a person and as a leader. Contemplating this issue is what allows you to change behaviors and renew yourself.

When the Worst Happens

We've already alluded to some of the learning this passage affords, from resiliency to self-knowledge. Let's look at some more specific knowledge you can glean from this passage that will increase your leadership intelligence:

- *Recognition that "playing the game" may result in losing.* In some companies, people advance who please everyone and offend no one. They assume that if they satisfy the system, they'll be successful. This is often true, to a point, but outstanding leaders manage the tendency, if they have it, to try to please and satisfy everyone. Instead, they say, do, and convey what they believe is right, working to manage conflict with others who disagree. Being passed over or forced to leave a company can initiate a new way of thinking about the requirements of leadership: *attempting to satisfy others is not leadership.* As one very well-known and outstanding CEO said to us recently, looking back on the moment early in his career when he was fired, "That was when I started to think for myself."

- *Knowledge of how to build your survivor muscles.* Getting passed over or fired is a more common occurrence today than ever before. The best leaders learn how to make it through this passage with their self-esteem and relationships intact. Instead of burning bridges by venting their rage at a boss, they remain professional throughout a difficult time. They become survivors who live to fight another day. Surviving downturns, technological changes, financial crises, and unexpected events besides being fired is a skill all leaders need, especially at senior levels.

- *Understanding of how to add another layer of depth.* All the passages deepen you as a leader, but this is the one where you are most likely to become more thoughtful, empathetic, and insightful. Someone once said that how much we learn is directly related to how much we suffer, and this adage applies here. Being fired from a job you love is gut-wrenching. Up until this point, you may have never experienced anything at work or in your career that has caused you so much anguish. The suffering makes you think and feel in ways you've never thought and felt before. At the time this happens, it's painful. Later on, though, it gives you a sense of perspective about work and appreciation for what other people are going through. Be open to the painful thoughts and feelings, and you'll develop into the type of well-rounded leader that someone who has never lost a job can't be.

Of all the professional passages, this is one where it's most difficult to see the opportunity hidden by the adversity. Trust us; it exists, and we have the stories of hundreds of executives to prove it. Perceived failure is a powerful catalyst for change. If you are patient, reflective, and willing to talk about this difficult experience, development as a leader emerges.

10

Being Part of an Acquisition or Merger

If you are a child of divorce and have had to adapt to a step-parent, you know something about this passage. When another organization acquires or merges with your company, you experience a sense of dislocation and disorientation. The family you've known for years has changed. All your assumptions, all your achievements, and all your relationships within that family are up for grabs. Not only might you have to adjust to a new boss but a new set of values and practices must be learned as well.

What's more, your place in the family is threatened. Whether the threat is real or perceived doesn't matter. There's an old saying about mergers: 1 plus 1 equals 1. In the new entity, positions are duplicated, and you may assume that you or your counterpart will soon be gone. This fear can make it difficult to lead effectively, especially in the initial, post-merger period. You're waiting for the other shoe to drop, wondering when and if it's going to happen. It's difficult to concentrate on business when you're concerned that you or half your colleagues will soon be fired. Unfortunately, this is often a time of intense work requirements. In the wake of a merger, there is much to do and so little time to do it.

Leaders learn how to function effectively under pressure during this passage and, at the same time, grow in other ways. To help you take advantage of this learning, it helps to prepare for what takes places when companies merge or are acquired.

Rejoining the Corporation

Leaders who have never been through this process before tend to underestimate its impact. Though you may grasp how the company will change quantitatively—fewer people, a new mix of resources, a different brand—you may not realize the psychological impact it will have on you. If you're an ambitious leader who has set a career path for yourself within an organization, you're going to be shocked to discover that this path no longer exists.

All the great performance reviews you've enjoyed, all the goals you've reached, all the connections you've made, all the promises that have been made to you—an acquisition or merger can invalidate these achievements and commitments. Psychologically, this can be difficult to deal with. It's even more difficult if the company that acquires you is a competitor, as is often the case. For a number of years, you've viewed the acquiring company as the enemy; you've made it a point to emphasize your strengths versus their weaknesses in internal and external communications. Now you are being asked to embrace their products, services, policies, and culture.

In addition, a merger or acquisition doesn't happen overnight. You're going to feel the impact for months, starting with the first rumor that the merger will take place. Many times, companies talk about how quickly and smoothly their merger went, boasting that it was completed in twenty-seven days. It may be that the legal process took twenty-seven days or that this was the amount of time needed to evaluate and reduce staff and other redundant operations. But in reality, the cultural adaptation process takes much longer. Phase I of a merger or acquisition is where everyone's time, energy, and focus go. This phase is when all the contractual and financial issues are addressed and decisions are made regarding people and operations. Phase II, however, is frequently overlooked. This is when the two cultures are brought together, when the hearts-and-minds issues are addressed. Leaders are suddenly forced into what William Bridges has termed "the neutral zone," that is, where a former identity, role, or self-concept ends and they are still undecided whether to fully commit to the new organization, enabling the formulation of a new identity. The place between these two events is confusing, emotional, and characterized by emotional highs and lows. Some people move quickly through the neutral zone (see Figure 10.1); others inhabit it for weeks, months, and occasionally years.

This is very difficult to do if you haven't grieved the loss of the old company, and most organizations don't provide for a grieving process; most individuals don't recognize the need to let go on their own. As a result, you may offer your new bosses a verbal buy-in, but secretly you still view them as "they" and the old corporate entity as "we." When GE acquired RCA, they had RCA's leaders visit the GE training facility at Crotonville. When the RCA people arrived, GE executives presented them with GE T-shirts. The next day, the RCA group brought in boxes of RCA T-shirts for GE leaders. Although the RCA leaders may have made this gesture with the best of intentions, they were missing the point: things had changed; RCA was not an equal. Acquiring companies want to know that their new people are on the team. Too frequently, however, acquired leaders see their role differently. They want to add value and believe they can do so by pointing out the flaws in the

Figure 10.1 The Neutral Zone.

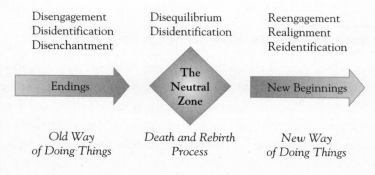

Source: Bridges, 1980.

acquirer's system, referring to their old system as a way to help them correct these flaws.

Exhibit 10.1 shows typical emotional responses to a merger; the responses progress through stages.

Exhibit 10.1. Emotional Response to a Merger.

Denial	"It won't happen."
Fear	"What will happen to me?"
Anger	"We've been sold out!"
Sadness	"Things used to be so much better."
Acceptance	"I guess we have no choice."
Relief	"This looks better than I thought at first."
Interest	"Maybe there are possibilities."
Liking	"I really feel comfortable now."
Enjoyment	"This could be great!"

Despite the best intentions on both sides, the offer to critique, change, or refer to former best practices is often not appreciated by the acquirer. The reason is that mergers and acquisitions are emotional events handled in a rational fashion. The learning for leaders occurs in managing their own reactions, developing an objective view of the change process, and eventually recognizing that lack of commitment doesn't make sense if you want to remain employed by the merged organization.

Learning More Than How to Keep Your Job

Making a successful transition from pre- to post-acquisition is an experience rich with learning, though on the surface it may seem like a survival exercise. You won't learn much, however, if you invest all your energy in just surviving. Although you certainly need to make the right connections with people in the new organization, this isn't your only responsibility. Some individuals are brilliant at surviving mergers and acquisitions, but this skill doesn't make them leaders; they're just good at keeping their heads down and looking like they're on board.

In previous chapters, we've saved the learnings for last. Here, we want to introduce you to them first because what you learn during this passage is more subtle than in some of the others. You'll be more motivated to take the actions we recommend later if you understand the five ways you can grow as a leader after an acquisition or merger:

1. *Figure out new rules quickly and start playing by them.* More than ever before, leaders need to transition from one set of rules to another. This is true, not only after mergers and acquisitions but in all sorts of other leadership situations—changing companies, working in another country, adjusting to a new CEO, and so on. After a merger or acquisition, your effectiveness is predicated on your ability to perceive what the new rules are about, how resources are acquired, how short cuts are taken, and how coalitions are formed. These rules may be quite different from what you're used to, and you need to be observant and ask questions in order to figure out the new system. The faster you're able to do this and incorporate what you learn into your standard operating procedures, the more successful you'll be as a leader.

2. *Remain a strong leader despite your sense of vulnerability.* This is a tough lesson for many leaders to learn, but an acquisition or merger is a powerful teacher. Many top executives we've worked with have told us that in the wake of these events, they feel like someone has taken away their company, that they've lost their identity. In the past, their identity, sense of competence, even their leadership values were directly derived from their company role. They took great pride in their company's reputation, market position, and culture, and their leadership style reflected the company's style. When the company changed virtually overnight, both this identification and their self-confidence were immediately eroded. Without their established identity, many executives feel vulnerable and weak, even wounded.

I think leaders who do not expose themselves to their people,
who don't make themselves vulnerable to their people, can't
effectively lead because people aren't going to think you are real.
If you shoot the messenger, that's going to elicit a certain kind of
response. If you are going to respond to disappointment instructively,
I think that's when people are with you forever. I think those are
great leadership moments.

JOSEPH BERARDINO, FORMER CEO, ANDERSEN WORLDWIDE

Learning to lead effectively with a wounded ego is a skill leaders need. An important part of leadership development that is rarely
taught in the classroom is the ability to manage one's ego in key situations. There are times when good leaders must recognize that a
direct report's idea is better than their own, that a customer's requirements supercede their own plans, or when negative feedback
from a peer is accurate. In other words, they must demonstrate
strength of character, even when they feel weak inside, and this passage facilitates the acquisition of this strength.

3. *Transcend the politics while focusing on the mission.* Politics
can be tremendously distracting. Although good leaders are aware
of political situations and know how to work effectively within
them, they don't become so enmeshed in jockeying for position
that they lose sight of their group or company objectives. Politics
always accelerates after a merger or acquisition. Great leaders
maintain their focus despite the political maneuvering. This is a
good skill to have, in that it's easy to become distracted from your
mission by politics, even when no merger or acquisition has taken
place. In all companies, politics—the informal negotiation and
exchange of power and influence to achieve outcomes—is a way
of life, and the high-performing leaders don't eschew politics; they
handle it with both integrity and flexibility. No matter what's happening around a good leader—loss of resources, removal of a key

supporter, setback from a client or customer—she continues to drive toward key goals.

4. *Maintain an open mind.* People are tempted to become defensive after their company is acquired. We see this often in coaching leaders through the acquisition process. An us-versus-them mentality develops, and more than one leader thinks to himself or says to others, "This is not as effective as the way we used to do things around here." It's natural to be close-minded initially; your feelings of betrayal have an impact on your perceptions. Gradually, however, the post-merger environment provides you with opportunities to grasp that "the new guys" aren't so bad. Many executives we've interviewed who have gone through this passage talk about an "Aha!" moment that occurs when they realize they have more in common with the new senior management and their culture than they realized. This can be a gradual realization or a sudden, shocking one, and it helps them understand that they should not hold tight to assumptions that may prove to be invalid. Open-mindedness is a quality that leaders can develop in other passages, but living through an acquisition or merger accelerates this ability, opening people up to other ways of running a business.

5. *Create a new network.* Again, this is a skill that leaders can acquire in other passages, but after a company changes hands, the need for building a new network is critical. It's a different

One of the things a leader learns in a crisis is to think more about whether people are really with you emotionally as well as intellectually. Intellectually, most people are smart, and they are part of the game and they know what you are going to report. But that's not enough. I think you need people with you emotionally. That takes time. You don't do that in memos, and you don't do that in meetings. You do that spending time one-on-one with people, getting to know them. In terms of bringing people along, you need to spend time with them on a human level.

JOSEPH BERARDINO, FORMER CEO, ANDERSEN WORLDWIDE

relationship-building challenge from those in other contexts, especially for leaders who have been at one company for years and have never experienced a merger or acquisition. Becoming adept at internal networking is an increasingly important skill for leaders in virtual or matrixed organizations.

Rebuilding a network is also necessary within a volatile business climate in which downsizings, re-sizings, and acquisitions are typical. We have worked with companies in which associates have lost their mentors and allies in a matter of months through downsizing or transfers, or when people resign to take other jobs. In these instances, it's incumbent on leaders to find other sources of support and sponsorship.

Getting on Board with One Foot

Andrew is a great example of someone who gradually learned these five lessons after his company merged, but he's also an example of someone who initially resisted these lessons because of the adversity he encountered in this passage.

Andrew had just been promoted to vice president of risk management when the board of his bank decided to merge with a larger financial institution. For ten years, Andrew had worked at this large bank in a variety of roles. The merger with the larger bank took place as part of the consolidation in the banking industry; most banks created growth through acquisition of new franchises, geographies, and customers. Andrew's bank had a strong culture, and he was proud of the company and his accomplishments within it during his tenure. He was one of a number of executives who were against the merger, although the board did not solicit his input.

Three months after the deal was closed, over one thousand people were fired from both banks, the majority from Andrew's company. Andrew survived, though three people in his risk management team and his boss did not. New policies and procedures were introduced, most of which Andrew didn't like; they seemed overly bureaucratic and process-oriented, even for someone in risk management. Andrew was even more disturbed, however, at feeling un-appreciated, as if he had to prove himself all over again. His opinions were not sought, and when he offered them, he felt that he had less credibility than those who had worked in the acquiring bank. Nonetheless, he tried to "fit in" (again, his words). He attempted to go along with the consolidations, changes, and new strategies, though almost every night he'd come home and complain to his partner about "how the company isn't like it was." He also regularly talked to his old boss, and they spent most of their conversation complaining.

Finally, Andrew sought the advice of a coach, and in their initial meeting told him he was contemplating resigning. His coach, however, after listening to Andrew's complaints and sharing his knowledge of the bank and its management group, suggested that Andrew might want to give it a little more time.

It took another month before Andrew's feelings of alienation and betrayal began to dissipate. One of the risk assessment projects he was working on went well, and he received several public compliments from officers he did not know well in the acquiring bank. As a result, he was invited to serve on an integration team, working on a vision for the merged company. Andrew began the process of contributing to the new organization in a substantial way and found the evolving vision created in the project team to be insightful, not all that different from how he viewed the organization's future. Soon Andrew found himself getting to know other executives from the former bank and maintaining his focus on the company's mission. Within a year, he had reestablished himself with solid performance and output, and he began to trust a new network of peers and fellow executives.

This scenario repeats itself in every merger or acquisition, and the key component is development of trust. Effective leaders learn to develop trust quickly, and even trust others before they have earned it, especially since many companies today operate virtually or they continually reorganize. Creating trust requires a positive attitude about other people and their intentions, and there is no better place to learn this critical leadership skill than in the midst of a merger.

Growing as a Company Changes

To maximize your leadership development in this passage, you need to combine some practical steps with some soul searching. Let's look at how you can do so:

- *Determine if you should remain with the new company.* As we noted earlier, this means not reacting too quickly to imposed changes. You need, instead, to objectively assess whether the new entity's values truly clash with something you hold important. If, for instance, you value straightforward and confrontational communication, and the new culture embodies passive, indirect consensus, your leadership talents may not be valued. Beginning to unhook may be the best option. It's difficult to grow as a leader and obtain the commitment of your team in a culture whose values you disavow; your anger at how the company operates will stand in the way of learning about your own effectiveness. Be sure, though, that it's the company's values you're at odds with rather than those of a new boss. In the majority of situations, you'll find a correspondence between your values and those of a new entity. Discovering this correspondence will make it easier for you to make the transition and focus on your new business goals.

> Your commitment has to be real. If it can't be real, why would you want to spend your life doing that? If it can't be real at work, why would you spend more time at work than you do at home? I think it's a shame when companies expect something that's different than who you are. I think a lot of organizations do try to tell you the truth. I think it's a question of finding that alignment between your style, your values, and the culture you see and the company that offers it.
>
> BILL GEORGE, FORMER CHAIRMAN AND CEO, MEDTRONIC

• *Work at assessing and expressing how you feel about the merger or acquisition.* In other words, don't try to tough it out and keep all your disappointment and animosity bottled up inside. Years after a merger took place, some executives still lament the event and wistfully describe the old organization in glowing terms. Stuck in the past, they remain closed to new information and ideas and fail to embrace the diversity of experience that enhances their leadership. Therefore, be honest with yourself and with at least one trusted adviser about your perspective on the merger or acquisition. If you fear that it means the end of your career or that you've wasted the last ten years, acknowledge this fear and make it explicit. The sooner you do, the faster you'll free yourself to take advantage of whatever opportunities exist in your post-merger environment.

• *Reconnect to the company.* We've talked about this earlier as a learning, but it's not something that you'll learn if you approach it passively. We coach executives working in a merged company to move beyond their immediate boss and develop a broader network. To build an influenced network, leaders need to put in a certain amount of personal time with people at different levels and in different areas to forge real relationships. This doesn't happen overnight, nor does it happen without a certain amount of awkwardness; you may think you're too old or too veteran to be engaging in networking. People also complain, "I worked for years to establish my network, and what good has it done me?" This is precisely the point. You need to be skilled at not just building one network but in rebuilding it and updating it. Leaders must be adept at connecting and re-connecting with people in a continuously changing organization.

• *Keep the lines of communication open with your direct reports.* At a minimum, effective leadership is focusing on the needs of your followers, and your team is as affected by the merger or acquisition as you are. Leadership requires helping them with the transition just as (ideally) your boss helps you with it. Focusing on the requirements of your team members will actually help develop your commitment to the new company. Talk to them, listen to them, keep them informed, and address their concerns. They need your support, and you need their support to accomplish the new goals that have emerged in the post-acquisition period.

• *Be patient.* Patience is indeed a virtue, especially today. Action-oriented, driven leaders are frequently quick to react to events; they form opinions and launch initiatives in response to new stimuli. In the wake of an acquisition or merger, patience may be the best strategy for adaptation. In fact, mergers take months or even years to achieve stability. For a leader, it takes time to learn the ropes, to make the connections, to appreciate the new people with whom you're working. You can't charge forward as you may have done in the past, and this can be frustrating. At the same time, it teaches you that waiting, observing, discussing, and thinking can yield positive results. After a merger, you have to develop other approaches to working and leading, at least for a while, and this process can be beneficial, especially if you've always made snap decisions and generally been a perpetual-motion executive. A little patience goes a long way in helping you deal more effectively with direct reports, as well as in assessing situations with greater objectivity.

Despite all this, most leaders respond negatively to news of a merger or acquisition. The key to learning in this passage is moving beyond the initial, negative reaction and being alert for career and educational opportunities. The other company involved in the transaction is involved because the combination offers unique value to customers, clients, and shareholders. The acquiring company in almost every case is buying talent, along with brand, technology, market share, products, and services. Recognizing that you are part of the asset being purchased may help you reframe your perceptions.

Remember, too, that they may offer you more opportunities to develop than your old organization. Obviously, the combined entity is bigger, but there may be many more hidden assets—those not readily apparent: intelligent people, new ways of doing things, creative ideas, change-oriented leaders, performance culture, and visionary thinkers, to name just a few. They may be in a better market position; they may have better training programs; they may have more overseas positions; they may have a culture or strategy that is well suited to the way you lead and manage. Many leaders we have coached during mergers observed much later that not only did they join a better company but they became a better leader in the process.

Equally important, this passage plays itself out when leaders acquire another company. In fact, the personal aspects of leading a merged entity can be even more challenging than the demands of being acquired. Leaders especially must keep their egos in check, listen openly, and learn to trust new people who are now working for them. They must be careful not to revert to established ways of doing things because "I'm in charge here now," or "speed demands it," or "these guys just don't get it," or, even worse, "we've won." The ability to objectively choose the best people, build a team, establish a vision, and gain the trust of others are leadership skills acquired in acquiring others.

Keep our opening analogy in mind when trying to process your feelings about the acquisition or merger. Going through a divorce is tough, but as hurt and abandoned as you might feel, be aware that your new stepparent might be a good person who could actually help you grow in ways not even possible in your old family.

11

Living in a Different Country or Culture

Previous sections have focused on adversity and diversity of professional experience. Now we'll address these topics from the personal side.

As you consider these personal passages, remember that it's actually impossible to separate the personal and the professional. Years ago, many companies required that leaders keep their personal life out of the office. Many executives in the fifties, sixties, and seventies believed that what went on at the office should always be left there and not affect family or other relationships. Today we know that such a separation is impossible, at least psychologically and emotionally. If you're going through a divorce or, in the case described in this chapter, your family accompanies you on an international assignment and does not adjust well, your focus and energy will be affected. By the same token, a career, job, or assignment that does not provide challenge, fun, and fulfillment will have a negative impact on your relationship with your spouse or partner over time.

The good news is that a personal passage is also an opportunity to grow and learn, both as an individual and as a leader. In our research, many executives fortunate enough to be posted outside their home country describe this particular passage as one of the most meaningful, transformational experiences in their lives. Whether they moved to a different country for work or simply lived abroad on their own, the immersion in a different culture caused them to look at all aspects of their life from a fresh perspective. You no doubt know someone who returned from time abroad a changed person—more reflective, more open-minded, and more aware of his or her values and priorities. These insights and perspectives can also occur when people don't leave the country but spend time in any "foreign" environment; they move from their affluent suburban home to teach and live in the inner city, or they move from the city to live and work in a rural area. In Action Learning leadership development programs, we work to create these types of experiences, for example, by taking highly paid executives into the inner city for two days to work in an AIDS clinic or build a home with Habitat for Humanity. Effective leadership development challenges assumptions and traditional ways of viewing the world and are often designed to achieve that effect. But experiences that challenge and stretch are available to leaders throughout their lives if they resolve not to become prisoners of their own experience. Nothing embodies this more than living for some time in a different country. Although we are looking primarily at geographically foreign experiences, everything we write about applies to immersion in any culture that is alien to your day-to-day experience.

The Challenges of Making a Foreign Journey

Let's begin with a caveat: living abroad will not have much of an effect on your life or leadership if the experience is very similar to your past experience. Some senior executives go abroad and live in replicas of the same communities they left, working and socializing with people like themselves, eating at McDonald's, and never really exposing themselves to what makes a foreign culture foreign. Just living in another country isn't the point. The key is to fully experience the different culture.

Here is the ideal scenario describing how this foreign experience might unfold. You are asked to become a marketing manager in your company's Thailand division—your first international assignment. You're excited about the assignment, knowing that if you want to be a leader in a global organization, you will need global experience because those moving up all seem to have this particular ticket punched. Your spouse and three children participate in predeparture cross-cultural training and go with you to Bangkok, Thailand, even though your children, because of their ages, don't particularly relish leaving their friends and moving far away. As a result, you feel guilty about uprooting them. When you arrive, the first few weeks are filled with confusing situations and many frustrations. You find that your children are too advanced for their classes; they are bored in school and frustrated, so you search all over Bangkok for alternative educational venues. It's also lonely; you and your spouse feel isolated during the first few weeks, despite the hospitality of the head of the Thai company and his attempts to include you and your family in social activities. At one particularly low moment, your spouse wonders whether the decision to leave home was a mistake.

Just as problematic, you find that the business environment is different and, in your view, less sophisticated than what you left. Dealing with the Thai governmental bureaucracy is slow and frustrating. Just as aggravating is the way your Thai vendors respond to your requests for products and services. On the surface, they're accommodating and friendly, but you regularly find that the commitment or delivery they said would happen in one day still hasn't arrived after a week. Language issues, too, make it difficult to get points across clearly to Thai direct reports.

After a period of time, however, you and your family settle in. Though your spouse and children may not love being abroad, they stop complaining and start appreciating aspects of the new culture. You also begin to appreciate the challenges more than you're frustrated by them. You take pride in the way you recognize what it takes to get requests honored; you form a new network that operates differently from the one you enjoyed back home, and you adapt your leadership style to the demands of the culture. You recognize the subtleties of communication that make all the difference in the Thai business world. Although at first you felt the Thai way of doing business was hopelessly complex and inefficient, you learn to appreciate their adaptability and genius for surmounting obstacles.

When you return home, you discover that not only do you have a greater appreciation for cognitive diversity—for people who think differently—but you're much calmer in the face of problems and better equipped to explore and identify alternatives. Although you've gained a great deal of knowledge about how to do business in a foreign country, the larger gain is internal; you have a better sense of who you are, especially in contrast to what you have experienced. The struggles and new experiences of living abroad have been opportunities for reflection. When you were struggling to communicate with your Thai employees, you thought long and hard about why you were unable to connect. They understood English well enough, but you eventually determined that your unspoken arrogance was off-putting. You saw yourself through their eyes, and you weren't particularly impressed by what you saw. You learned how to project confidence without arrogance, expose some vulnerability, and appreciate and value individuals within the Thai culture. And that made a big difference in the way you related to others, as well as to your capability as a leader.

> I went to Asia as a multinational Regional Head with a pregnant wife, a troubled marriage, and a passport that had only been out of Canada three times and only to Europe. The fears of fatherhood, a failing marriage, and a career step beyond my experience and competence propelled me to work night and day to be successful. It was the true turning point in my career, and my Hong Kong-born daughters remain great joys.
>
> BILL CAMPBELL, CHAIRMAN, JPMORGAN CHASE CARD SERVICES

What to Avoid When Going Abroad

Like all the professional passages, it's not the event itself that makes or breaks you as a leader but your reaction to it. Moving into

a leadership role or receiving responsibility for a business can foster leadership growth only when you respond to these events in
a way that fosters self-development. Living abroad might have
no more impact on your leadership skills than moving to a new
house down the block. Perhaps you receive a unique opportunity
to open your company's new China office or spend a year traveling
throughout the Indian subcontinent. But if you spend this time
working, living, and thinking in the same way you always have, the
year will be wasted. We have worked with many executives both
abroad and at home. We have learned through our research that
when you live abroad, the following traps should be avoided in
order to grow as a leader:

• *Don't live in a bubble.* This trap is not as easy to avoid as it
might seem. When you're living in another country, you can easily
convince yourself that you're experiencing it fully, simply because
the sights and sounds around you are so foreign. If you're working
abroad, you may be interacting with employees from this new country, and their speech and dress and work style may reinforce the idea
that you are far from home. These superficial interactions, however,
aren't sufficient to provide you with fresh perspectives or appreciate diversity at a meaningful level.

Many of us have a bubble-wrap reflex when we encounter a foreign culture, and it makes us uncertain and uncomfortable. It may
not be a conscious decision to isolate and protect ourselves from the
differences of the culture, but that is the net effect. We once knew
a CEO for a major corporation who was visiting operations in
Poland, and his Polish hosts wanted to give him a taste of the food
and entertainment of their country. They threw a lavish evening
party that was true to their Polish traditions, and that went on
for quite a while. Finally, they took the CEO to the airport so he
could board his jet and fly to another country for meetings the next
day. Just before they arrived at the hangar, they passed a new
McDonald's, and the CEO said, "Why the hell didn't we just go
to McDonald's? It was on the way to the airport anyway." This

antipathy toward other cultures is not unique to this CEO. His preference for the familiar, his emphasis on saving time, and his subtle contempt are surprising only because they were expressed so openly.

• *Don't be a prisoner of your own experience.* When you have the opportunity to live abroad, be aware of your reflex to isolate yourself from the culture. To maintain this awareness, ask yourself the following simple questions:

> The dawn of a new marriage, a new career in Financial Services, and now an adopted daughter have just made me comfortable with whatever successes I have achieved and leadership I have provided. Life is a journey and business success can be an outcome, but it is seldom the driver.
>
> BILL CAMPBELL, CHAIRMAN, JPMORGAN CHASE CARD SERVICES

Do I regularly eat local food at local restaurants?

Do I seek out and accept invitations to stay in people's homes who are native to the country?

Do I take advantage of opportunities to travel in the host country and visit important cultural, religious, and political landmarks?

Do I regularly try to communicate with all different types of people in this country?

Do I work to establish trusting, open friendships with some people in this country that will outlast my assignment?

If I'm in the country as part of a work assignment, do I make an effort to meet people who have nothing to do with work?

Do I make an effort to learn the country's customs and history through observation and conversation?

Do I shop at local stores, socialize with people who are native to the country, and generally try and live as the people in the country do?

Do I use my awareness of cultural differences to better understand the culture from which I came?

Finally, if you're living abroad because of a work assignment, recognize that an international business class has emerged and that you're still in the bubble if you limit your experiences to this business class. Our colleague, Stephen Rhinesmith, has noted that an executive at the top of most large global corporations anywhere in the world probably has more in common with other senior global executives than with a farmer in his or her own country. Because of global business practices, extensive use of English as a business language, and constant movement around the world in a cocoon of first-class air travel, restaurants, hotels, and offices, a global business class has emerged that is less identified with its own country than with other members of the class. Living on a farm in their own country might be more enlightening for these people than traveling throughout the world and not experiencing it.

How to Take Advantage of a Once-in-a-Lifetime Opportunity

Breaking your frame of reference is not an easy task, but living in a foreign culture facilitates achieving this objective. Many business executives grow up in a corporation and develop strong, unconscious cultural biases. They are frustrated, surprised, and sometimes daunted to see first-hand that despite their relative sophistication about business and the world, out-of-awareness cultural values can impede communication, decision making, and the effort to lead people. They have experienced what CDR International Partner Stephen Rhinesmith, terms the "Epcot Center version of cross-cultural experiences," that is, moving quickly through countries and observing differences is similar to the experience of moving through cultural pavilions at Disney World's Epcot Center; the reality of living for some time in a country different from one's own can create deep, fundamental change, both personally and professionally.

We all operate with certain assumptions about our companies, competitors, markets, and industries. It takes a frame-breaking experience—a direct challenge to these assumptions—to develop into a better leader. The professional passages create this adjustment in certain ways, and living abroad does it in another way. If you take full advantage of your time abroad, you'll emerge with an expanded capacity for seeing things from multiple perspectives and an ability to work effectively with people who have ideas and approaches very different from your own.

To capitalize on your foreign experience, do the following:

• *Adopt an adventurer's mind-set.* Be willing to try new things, to take reasonable risks, to explore areas and ideas that you find the most foreign. This doesn't mean that you should put yourself in physical danger but that you should test yourself in other ways. If you're in an Asian country, it may mean spending time touring a Buddhist monastery or taking a class in meditation from a monk. If you're in South America, it may mean taking a weekend trip down a river through an ancient rainforest. In the business world, it may mean working hard to communicate your ideas to others in a different language, working differently with customers or suppliers, and listening hard so you understand their ideas.

This type of communication takes time and effort. It may take you days and scores of questions to comprehend a complex distribution system or assess why their unique sales strategy is so effective. At times, you will feel foolish and ignorant because you have to ask so many questions, and it takes you so long to figure things out. An adventurer, though, is willing to endure a bit of hardship for the sake of exploration and discovery. Leaders who view living abroad as a career stepping-stone are conservative in how they approach a different culture; they let their anxiety about being different, vulnerable, or visible keep them detached. They get much less out of the experience than those who view it as an adventure.

• *Learn first; teach second.* Some people approach foreign assignments, especially ones in less-developed countries, with an unconscious defensive attitude of superiority. They believe they have much to offer and others have little to offer them in return. This can also be true for people who live abroad for other reasons, from volunteers to missionaries, and much cross-cultural training today is designed to help people uncover these attitudes before they depart. They intend to manage a different culture rather than experience it. As a result, their time abroad becomes a self-fulfilling prophecy; they do give a lot and receive very little.

No matter whether you're living in a developing country, a major industrial power, or somewhere in between, it's best to operate on the premise that a new culture has a great deal to teach you. This is easy to remember when entering a new culture, because excitement and enthusiasm are predominant. It is after a year or two that subtle contempt can set in. Force yourself to keep an open mind, especially if you become frustrated with what is different and begin to long for the familiar. Your view might be that your host country is backward or unsophisticated, and this judgment prevents you from grasping the underlying cultural values and differences that constitute the context in which you are now living. If you're open to learning and make an effort to observe and listen, you'll find alternatives to your standard operating procedure.

We know a CEO of one of this country's largest corporations, and we'll call him Frank. A number of years ago, his company gave him a tough European assignment. Frank was designated a "high talent" within the company, always successful, always in control; he could have easily approached the assignment with the idea of mastering and controlling his new environment. Instead, he recognized that he didn't understand the subtleties of the European country to which he was assigned, and before he issued a single directive or suggested any changes in the status quo, he listened and observed. More than that, he spent weekends traveling throughout Europe, attempting to get a feel for the people and the culture that he would never get in his company's offices. By the end of his time there, he had not only earned the respect of his employees, he had adapted his ideas and strategies to his new culture. This ability to adapt served Frank well. When he returned to the United States, he continued to be promoted; his ability to read situations, intuit subtle differences in attitudes, and respond in a flexible way served him well as a leader.

- *Function effectively without knowing the rules or how to behave.* This is great practice for when you return to your home country. Today, because of globalization and the constant homogenization induced by global media, in almost every large organization in every country, business rules and practices are rapidly changing. Leadership models such as openness, operational metrics such as Six Sigma, practices such as longer workdays with shorter lunch breaks—are converging and continuously shifting with each new trend or technological breakthrough. Leaders can't wait for clarity and for all the answers to emerge before they act. Instead, they need to get things done with limited information, all the while assimilating and assessing and adapting their policies as new data emerge.

Working in a foreign country provides training for assimilating, assessing, and adapting skills. Most people worry about committing a business or social faux pas because they don't know the customs. They also become concerned about seeming incompetent because they don't know how to navigate foreign bureaucracies, the transportation system, or even something as simple as ordering food at a restaurant.

When you're in these situations, don't panic. More important, don't fear exposing your lack of knowledge by saying, "I don't know" or by being reluctant to ask "dumb" questions. For leaders, the ability to expose one's vulnerabilities by admitting to "not knowing" is a skill that creates a learning environment for others in any context. In a different country, as a leader you can practice the "don't know everything" response and try to learn what you need to know and be willing to make mistakes. Order steak in a restaurant, receive a fish stew, and resolve to either try something new or learn the right words for what you want. Similarly, if you request a marketing plan and your direct report provides you with a plan that contains all manner of sidebars, digressions, or tangential information, don't give in to frustration. Pay attention instead to the sidebars and digressions and see if that's your direct report's way of providing you with information you really need.

Through Action Learning programs and other global leadership training experiences, we've witnessed the positive impact of a foreign sojourn when people do the right things. Even though Action Learning only provides a short-term situation (a few weeks or a month in another country), it delivers long-term results. The program is purposely designed to force executives to rely on their own resources; they have to make their own travel plans and living arrangements, as well as meet a business challenge by figuring out the modus operandi of businesses and people in their country. Companies like Johnson & Johnson, GE, Novartis, and Diageo have similar global programs, deliberately placing their executives in countries where they don't know the language, forbidding them some of the common support tools, and generally subjecting them to the adversity experienced by any first-time traveler to another land. This adversity demands that people gather information, be creative, and think through accepted practices and beliefs.

When You Return Home

Think about the first time you visited another country on your own. Perhaps you went to Europe when you were in college or went on an adventure such as backpacking in the Andes. Maybe you joined the Peace Corps or spent a year working for Habitat for Humanity. Even if these experiences took place many years ago, you probably still recall the cultural shock, especially when you returned home. We've talked to many people—executives as well as nonbusiness people—about what they got out of these experiences, and they've noted a number of the learnings we've mentioned: greater appreciation of diversity, the ability to see things from a fresh perspective, and so on. Here are two other common reactions to what is learned:

• *Insights about who you are and why you do what you do.* Living abroad is a wake-up call. It rings an alarm about unexamined beliefs and behaviors and suggests how so much of both are culturally based. When travelers return home, they can see these beliefs and behaviors from a new perspective and often rethink them.

• *Increased tolerance for vulnerability and loneliness.* Being in another culture for a sustained period of time is often a lonely feeling; leaders are cut off from familiar people and places. As we've noted, it's also a time when circumstances force individuals to admit their lack of knowledge. When they return home, they're better able to deal with the vulnerability and loneliness of both life and leadership.

Be aware, too, that returning home causes some people to react negatively to their home environment. Especially after spending a few years living abroad in a diverse society, they return to their monocultures and find them unspeakably dull. They have come to appreciate the differences rather than the similarities among people, and uniform thinking and consensus bore them. Studies have documented that returning executives are especially vulnerable to leaving their company on re-entry because the company does not recognize or credit their experiences abroad, acknowledge the changes they have experienced, or offer them heightened challenges.

For leaders, this reaction can be an impetus for change. In some cases, people request that their companies give them another foreign assignment, or they look for a new job or even a new career that satisfies their desire for diversity.

In most instances, though, the impact is one of increased growth and maturity. It's possible that others may not appreciate this growth and maturity. Your company, for instance, may not appreciate your fresh perspective and increased tolerance for diversity. Other companies, however, will recognize that you're the type of leader who is desperately needed for success in a global marketplace.

12

Finding a Meaningful Balance Between Work and Family

Paradoxes reside in many passages, but the paradox of balancing work and family is especially challenging. (We use the term *family* to refer to any meaningful support system, including partners and friends.) Much has been written on this subject and on the related issue of balancing the professional and the personal, but unlike many leadership educators and coaches, we don't believe balance is possible. If your goal is to strike an equal, ideal balance between work and family, you'll fail. If you attempt to give your company forty hours of your time every week and your partner and kids forty hours, you'll probably end up satisfying no one. In fact, if you choose to be a senior executive in most large global companies today, because of the nature of competition, real balance is prohibited by your choice to accept this challenging assignment. The paradox is that a real balance isn't possible, but a relative one is.

In today's world of work, one area of your life is going to suffer. At times, you'll make certain sacrifices for your career and organization, and in other situations you'll make sacrifices for your family. Imbalance is the norm. The key, therefore, is to achieve a meaningful balance, a dynamic balance—one that is flexible and situational. In other words, you and your family reach consensus about what's required for your job and what's required for your family, and you try to adhere to these guidelines as best you can. You may be spending an inordinate amount of time in the office during strategic planning and budgeting or conducting year-end reviews, but you've discussed this issue in advance with your family, and they accept a temporary suspension of the rules. You may also decide to limit the amount of time you spend on work and accept that this might limit your career.

A meaningful balance is meaningful to you personally. Joe and his family may be willing to accept that he's going to be traveling extensively during the next ten years and will miss some birthdays and anniversaries and kids' baseball games, whereas Janet and her family are unwilling to accept as much travel or as many missed events. Families need to define "balance" together.

This passage is an opportunity to arrive at a definition of balance. Most of the time, people enter it because a life or work event has caused them to turn inward and focus on the meaning of family and work. Perhaps their spouse has asked for a trial separation, or they've been terminated, and they've asked themselves, "Why am I doing what I'm doing?" and "Is my career really worth it?" For many in the United States, the events of 9/11, 2001, created this type of self-reflection and stock taking.

To make sure this passage is a time of growth and learning, we'd like to give you a sense of what takes place internally and externally as people deal with these and other questions.

Becoming Conscious of Balance

This passage tends to arise later rather than sooner. Young executives are usually very ambitious and willing to work long hours. Recently graduated MBAs who work for top consulting firms often accept, even relish, total demands on their time. Consulting companies often provide free dinners to young professionals in an effort to encourage them to work longer and harder. These early-career professionals love the adrenaline rush of traveling around the world and the opportunity to put their education and ideas into practice. Many times, they're not even involved in relationships and are more than willing to sacrifice a personal life for professional gain.

Even if they have a partner, however, they often make it clear to that partner that work comes first.

Even executives in their thirties and forties may not become acutely conscious of the need for a meaningful balance. If they're married and have children, they and their spouses may agree that career and financial gain must be prioritized. Couples are often so focused on achieving specific goals—a certain size home in a certain community, private schools for children, vacations—that work becomes their means to an end.

At some point in midlife, though, all this changes. Sometimes a professional passage, such as a significant failure, triggers the change. Other times, it's a personal passage that is the catalyst—the loss of a loved one, for example. Whatever the cause, it creates a disconnect between the individual and his work. He gradually comes to question all the sacrifices he's made for a company and his career. He wonders if it was worth it to miss most of his kids' childhood or to endanger the relationship he has with his partner. He may even question all the time and energy he has invested in his job, thinking to himself, "There must be more than this." He questions whether he might do something more meaningful with his life than help sell products, whether relationships with the people he cares most about or establishing a spiritual connection are more important than the job. Even though all this questioning can cause him to quit, the typical outcome is a desire to achieve a more meaningful balance between work and family.

Some people, of course, wake up to discover they've emphasized family to the detriment of their careers. They chose not to travel as much or work as many hours as their companies wanted. They may have refused to relocate because they didn't want to uproot their families or chosen positions that demanded less of them but offered fewer career rewards. At some point, they realize that the people they went to business school with or with whom they worked at their first jobs are now several levels ahead of them, and they become frustrated. They may even start questioning the balance between work and family because they can't afford the things that other, more successful executives can afford.

Realistically, however, most people go through this passage because they've invested more in work than family; some women are the exception to this rule. Relatively early in their careers, they're faced with the choice of whether they should start a family. This may entail taking six months or six years off from work. In either case, they often find that it's difficult to pick up where they left off. In addition, still relatively few women with children are in senior leadership positions. Though this is starting to change, some corporate leaders believe that women with children simply can't make a total commitment to work.

Although these attitudes are understandably aggravating to women, our point is that they tend to struggle with the work-family balance issue earlier than men. Increasingly, some women "solve" this problem when their husbands agree to be stay-at-home dads. In other instances, women decide to have children later in life. Still others rely on professional child-care providers and avoid a sustained work absence. No matter what option women choose, this passage is often even more intense for them than it is for men, and the struggle to achieve a meaningful balance can go on for years. Cultural norms, as well as friends and relatives, can make women feel tremendously guilty for entrusting their children to nannies and au pairs.

Whether you're a woman or a man, you enter this passage torn by the natural desire to find both work and family fulfillment. Complicating matters is organizational encouragement to achieve work-family balance. Everyone from the CEO to your boss may encourage you to take all your vacation time and be home every night for dinner with your family. No doubt, they mean it. Unfortunately, work realities render their good intentions meaningless. Companies want their people to achieve this balance but not if the work product suffers. Organizations will take as much of an employee's life as he is willing to give, and this makes perfect sense. As humanistic as it might seem on the surface to insist that people spend more time

with their families, it's not humanistic to downsize the workforce—
a consequence if productivity falls because people aren't spending
sufficient time on the job.

We know of one highly accomplished executive whose wife suffered from a serious illness. The company was very understanding
and encouraged this executive to spend the time he needed with his
wife. He did so, and one week before Christmas, he was terminated.
He simply wasn't able to maintain an acceptable level of productivity, and when the review of his performance against his peers was
made, the other factors were not deemed relevant.

As brutal as it sounds to say so, this executive made a choice
about work-family balance, and despite the negative consequences,
it was the right one for him, and he felt good about it. His values
dictated that he care for the most important person in his life during her time of need, even if it meant he would lose his job. As we'll
see, values are critical for resolving the work-family paradox.

Calculating What You Will Tolerate

We cannot overemphasize that every individual has to determine
how much work-family imbalance she's willing to accept and the
price she's willing to pay. Some women, for instance, are willing to
forsake a family for their careers. For others, such a sacrifice is unacceptable. Similarly, some executives will sacrifice time with their
family early in their career but not later. Others will jump through
every hoop the organization places in their path, and their spouses
will support them as they jump.

The CEO of a large financial services company told us a story
about what happened to him in midcareer. For the sake of a significant promotion, he was asked to uproot himself, his wife, and his
three children and move across the country. He was willing to do so
because it was a great career opportunity, and his wife and children
were enthusiastic about having new experiences. As they were
driving across the country, following the moving truck with all their
belongings, this executive called in to his office and received the

message that the company had decided to move him to a different office. This meant selling the house they had bought, explaining to the children that they weren't going to the wonderful place with the lake and the beautiful weather after all, and dealing with the logistics of relocating twice in twenty-four hours. On top of that, this executive had to go through some serious mental gymnastics, as he wondered what the "real" reason was that management had decided to shift him to a different location. Despite everything, this future CEO didn't question his company's decision, let alone protest it, and his family remained supportive of him and the second move.

To many people, an event like this would have triggered the beginning of this passage and a questioning of work-life issues. Some executives would have resigned, or at least confronted their boss on being told in the middle of the drive to relocate again. It all depends on the individual and how much uncertainty and unpredictability he is willing to tolerate or how much his partner and children are willing to tolerate.

Perhaps the worst way to deal with this passage (and a way that many executives choose) is to deny that you're making sacrifices or that you'll have to pay a price for making them. If you're traveling around the world and working enormously long hours and thinking about or doing work when you're at home, you are not engaged and your family knows it. At the worst, your relationship is diminished. Your children feel distant from you or don't know you well.

Even at best, though, it can become an issue that creates ongoing tension in your relationships. Today most spouses expect that their partner will contribute to running the household and raising children, and if you contribute only minimally, you can expect to pay a price. This may be an acceptable price, but you need to think about this issue and discuss it with your partner. If you are in denial about it—if you rationalize why it is necessary for you to be a workaholic—you will be blindsided by the repercussions your choices entail.

Similarly, don't delude yourself that you can "multitask" your way out of this imbalance. We've coached incredibly busy senior executives who maintain that even though they work constantly at home, they also pay attention to their spouse and children and that even though they spend a significant percentage of their vacations with their computers and cell phones, there is still time to swim, golf, sightsee, and hike with their families. They admit that they spend inordinate amounts of time on work-related matters, but they add that when they are with their family, it's "quality time." This is generally nothing more than a rationalization. If they're not fully engaged and present when they are with their families (and it's difficult to be this way when every conversation is interrupted by a cell phone call from work), then they are simply fooling themselves into thinking they're providing their family with what they need.

Some people also deny that choosing family over work will have repercussions. As we've mentioned, some women find it extraordinarily difficult to resume their careers after having children. Whether this is unfair isn't the issue. Some women refuse to face the reality that having children can have a negative impact on their career. If they don't discuss this impact in advance with their partner as well as their boss, they may be surprised. If they convince themselves that nothing is going to change when they have children—the time they spend in the office, how others perceive their commitment to work, their work schedule flexibility—then they will struggle in this passage. One day, perhaps after an argument with their partner or a confrontation with their boss—they will realize they made a major decision without fully considering its implications.

Of course, it's not just women who choose family over work or try to achieve a perfect balance. We have coached and know male executives who absolutely refuse to miss certain events in their child's life, or they turn down great career opportunities because it would interfere with their family time. We know of one senior executive who arrived late at the company's annual top management meeting because it was more important for him to be at home for his son's birthday. This choice fits their values, but some of these men are tremendously resentful when they plateau at a

The thing that I've heard and I think that rings true to me
is about the fellow who ran Emerson Electric. I think his
name is McKnight. It was a very successful company for
many years. He said there are three great priorities in life
and they are your health, your family, and your work. He
would order the priorities: the first and foremost is your
health. If you are not maintaining your health, you are no
good to your family, your work, or yourself or anything else.
So your first priority is watching over your health. Your
second priority, he would say, is your family. The third
priority is your work. The trick is to devote the time to
your work such that you are able to give the first two
the time that is needed. That is where the tradeoff comes
because in your life, your work comes and goes and you
walk away and that's the end of that. If your whole life is
based on your work, you are in sad trouble. You've got
to be able to devote the time to it in order for it to be
successful. Every day you are making triage decisions.
I find that all the time. You are either disappointing
somebody at work, or you are disappointing a child, or
wife. You can't be lopsided in that. They need to understand and the business needs to understand that you
are balancing a lot of variables. The worst example of
this I think is today in the United States with the two-
breadwinner family where there are children. The women,
especially, have tremendous pressure on them and feel
tremendous guilt because they've got responsibilities to
themselves, to their parents, to their children, to their
spouse, to their job; there's never enough time to feel
satisfied. Part of this is just accepting that and not letting
it make you crazy. There is no easy out.

RAY VIAULT, VICE CHAIRMAN, GENERAL MILLS

certain level. They denied to themselves that their balancing act would have any consequences. Thus they enter this passage and become tremendously angry and resentful, failing to grasp how their actions resulted in the situation they're angry and resentful about. Rather than use this issue as a catalyst to learn about themselves and find a meaningful balance, they become mired in their negative emotions.

To maximize leadership learning and growth, therefore, don't deny; instead, do the following:

• *Let your values be your work-family guide.* Start out by asking yourself these questions:

How truly important is it to participate fully in your family's day-to-day activities? (Children learn in both ways: from parents who are present and from those who are absent.)

Do you believe marriage should involve an equal division of labor and child-raising responsibilities?

Do you believe in typical male-female marital roles? Is it possible you have feelings about roles that you aren't aware of or haven't articulated?

Can you achieve happiness and fulfillment only through reaching ambitious career goals?

These are the types of values-based questions you need to consider. As you enter this passage, you may feel as if the choice in front of you is impossible: Do you move your family to Saudi Arabia and advance your career, even though your family hates the idea of living there? You can't use logic to arrive at an answer; you can argue both sides of the proposition. Therefore, take some time out to reflect on what you really value. Admittedly, it is tough to reflect on this issue when you're working eighty hours per week, so you may need to spend a little time outside the work environment to come to terms with your values; you might escape to the country for a weekend or go on a long walk. A coach or another adviser may be able to facilitate this process, providing you with a sounding board to test what is really important to you. Some people value achieving capstone positions above all else, and in some situations their families will support them, no matter how much time and energy they must devote to this quest. Others value family to the point where they draw a line and refuse to cross it when it comes to working more than forty hours per week.

Dan, for instance, had P&L responsibility for a division of a large software company. His organization valued his knowledge and skills and accommodated his desire to spend as much time as possible with his family. When his company was bought, however, he had to deal with a new boss and a new set of people and procedures. As someone going through the professional passage of being acquired, Dan recognized that he should be creating a new support network. He realized he could use lunches and after-work social gatherings as ways to build this network, but he usually refused to take advantage of these opportunities. Dan ate lunch at his desk and worked so that he could arrive home to have dinner with his family every night. Because he wanted to be home at night, he went to very few after-work functions. Dan had incredibly strong family values, and he had vowed when he started working for this software company that he would not adopt a schedule that would prevent him from maintaining these values. In Dan's mind, he knew exactly how much he was willing to give his organization. Though he knew he was placing himself in a vulnerable position by not developing this network immediately, his behavior was dictated by his values, and he felt comfortable with his decision.

• *Involve your partner early on in your decisions about work and family*. Reach consensus on what you're willing to do for work and where you'll draw the line. Most people don't have these discussions until after the fact. When they do get around to talking about these issues, they usually take the form of arguments. Typically, one person misses a kid's concert or game or takes yet another ten-day trip or misses a birthday or anniversary, and this event triggers an argument in which promises are made and then broken later on. The time to talk is early in a career. At that point, you can create parameters that will help you create a meaningful balance.

• *Monitor your attitude toward success.* When you join a company, the organization shapes your perspective about success. In formal and informal ways, they communicate that your success revolves around promotions and that titles, perks, salaries, and bonuses are how you measure your achievements. If you accept this as gospel throughout your career, you'll find yourself asking, "Is this all there is?" at some point.

As you grow older and gain a diversity of life and work experiences, your notions about success usually change. You may not be aware of these changes, however, if you don't consciously think about this issue or talk to anyone about it. You may not realize that you consider raising emotionally healthy kids a greater achievement than achieving a certain organizational position. You may not grasp that your work with a community group gives you more satisfaction than your job-related work. Pay attention, therefore, to how your ideas about success are evolving. Don't let your new definition of success hit you like a ton of bricks during this passage. Revisit it at least once every year, and adjust your behaviors accordingly.

Experiencing the Rewards

We've focused on how people struggle to find a meaningful balance between work and family, but this passage can also be a highly rewarding experience. When people learn how to strike a meaningful balance, they acquire a strong sense of self. We don't want to become overly spiritual or poetic, but this balance confers a feeling of harmony, of living life in accordance with one's values and beliefs.

Some of the best leaders we've known live value-consistent lives. They have gone through this passage and found a way to meet business and personal goals. As a result, they project an inner confidence that makes others trust and respect them. They don't look or act like people whose lives are out of balance, who are obsessive workaholics or distracted by family problems. Instead, they are the kind of leaders of whom people say, "He really has his act together." This doesn't mean that he has struck the perfect balance between work and family because, as we've noted, there is no such thing. There are times when his spouse complains that he's traveling too much or when he feels guilty that he's taking a three-week vacation when he should be in the office. Most of the time, though, he has found a middle ground that allows him to satisfy the needs of his organization and his family. He has the aspect of a mature leader.

> I think the important thing is to try to take care of one's health and of the family. I try to take my holiday regularly. That's it.
>
> THOMAS EBELING, CEO, NOVARTIS PHARMACEUTICALS

Such a leader's maturation is due, in part, to receiving the support of his family. When you see Oscar winners or star athletes from winning teams attributing their success to the support they received from others, these statements of gratitude are usually heartfelt. Although there are exceptions, strong leaders generally have strong families or support systems. They are able to operate with certainty and purpose, in part because they know that no matter what happens, they can rely on their families for support.

Finally, people who go through this passage learn a lot about themselves and what really matters to them. Early in a career, many high-potential people are workaholics and devote themselves fully to their companies and careers. Even when they start families, they rationalize their workaholic tendencies, telling themselves there will be plenty of time later on to play with their kids and be with their partners. One day they realize that the time to be with their family is short. They discover that the distance between themselves and their family is too great to be bridged. For a number of years, they've been involved in a world of quick decisions, intense pressure, high-powered meetings, rewards for performance, and a jet-set corporate lifestyle. The other world of family is very different, and many executives seek shelter in their business cocoons from the slower-paced, delayed-gratification aspects of their personal lives. They may do this unconsciously, but at some point they realize they've separated their two worlds, and their partner and kids have grown in one direction while they've grown in another.

Ideally, you'll go through this passage and make an effort to close the gap between work and family before it becomes too wide. This is the time when many leaders set limits on their work time and schedules and have tough discussions with their partners about what is acceptable behavior. The effort is worth it, though, because people emerge from this passage with a firm sense of who they are and what's important in their lives, providing them with the inner strength that marks outwardly strong leaders.

13

Letting Go of Ambition

Despite the somber tone of its title, this passage connotes leadership maturity rather than resignation or reluctant acceptance. It's not a reaction to missed job opportunities or to being turned down for promotions. You aren't saying to yourself, "I just don't have what it takes. I guess I'll hang in there until retirement." It is instead about loving what you do, no longer having the urge to seek a "higher" position or enhance your credentials. Letting go of ambition is a kind of epiphany, because for the first time in your life, your work requirements and the job you hold are a perfect match. After years of strategizing about the next move and keeping one eye alert for the next opportunity, you have no interest in doing anything but what you're currently doing.

What "Letting Go" Means

The late Beatle George Harrison once said, "My ambition is to have no ambition." We suspect he was aspiring to a higher state of consciousness, as befits the most spiritual member of the group. People invest enormous amounts of energy mapping out their careers and developing skills that will increase their attractiveness as job candidates. They compete in corporate tournaments in which success is usually defined in terms of promotions, advancements, bigger budgets, more people, larger offices, or more impressive titles. This is fine, but at a certain stage it is no longer necessary. Many outstanding leaders reach a point in their lives in which the definition of success begins to shift. It is no longer about moving up but about mastery. Many people reach a point in their lives when they want to focus exclusively on what they are doing, and this is a sign of a leader operating at full capacity. All this individual's energy is focused on the job, and this focus can help him operate at peak effectiveness.

Letting go of ambition doesn't mean issuing a declaration to corporate leadership that you have arrived. In fact, we advise senior executives we work with *not* to share this insight about themselves with the people they work with, precisely because it can be easily misinterpreted. Instead, this passage is a process that takes place inside of you. Accordingly, it frees you to do what you love without concerns about how your job or career is being affected.

How the Process Works

Understandably, people don't like to admit that they've let go of their ambition for fear that their supervisor will assume they've lost their drive and desire to achieve goals. In fact, they often don't like to admit it to themselves. After years of continuous striving, it feels odd not to be driven to move on to the next big assignment. As a result, some people never experience this passage because they believe, almost obsessively, that they must keep seeking the next job or title, even though their heart is not in it. They are the ones who sometimes receive a promotion but look wistfully back at their previous job.

Letting go of ambition doesn't happen overnight. It is the result of years of experience and feedback. You realize that what everyone had told you about success isn't necessarily true. You discover that it is not a black-or-white proposition, that it's not just about winning and losing. Many of us grow up wanting to be CEOs or have some other highly ambitious career goal such as winning a Nobel Prize, being on the cover of *Fortune* magazine, or receiving a prestigious scientific award. Such goals are important, but sooner or later almost everyone comes to terms with the fact that they're not going to happen. In this passage, you come to terms with your aspirations. You accept that success is not just moving up but it is moving in place. You can achieve great things doing exactly what you've been doing and doing it better.

Learning to Love Being Second: Malcolm

Malcolm, for instance, has had a stellar career. An engineer by training, he ran a few smaller software companies and is now the chief technology officer for a large corporation. Earlier in his career, Malcolm had a "conqueror" mentality. He was highly ambitious and started two software firms with an eye toward challenging the giants of the industry. By the time he started up a third firm, however, Malcolm had learned that although he loved the product development process, he did not like the operational responsibilities of running a

---

I became less and less happy with my work, and I realized that I was spending all my time and energy in numbers and no real time working with people, working with customers, motivating employees, developing innovative new products—all the things I love to do. I was on the track to be CEO at Honeywell, and there were others, too. I thought about that, and I said if I get to be CEO, it's going to be five to seven years to get the company back to where it was, not to where I wanted it to be.

One day I was driving home after work, and I had this vision of being very unhappy at Honeywell and deciding to move on. I realized that this was all about chasing my ego to be CEO of this large corporation. When I faced myself in the mirror, I realized that Honeywell was changing me more than I was changing Honeywell.

BILL GEORGE, FORMER CHAIRMAN AND CEO, MEDTRONIC

---

business. He was not interested in selection, management meetings, or operational reviews. The financial details of the business bored him. He sold his last firm to his present employer, and during the first few months as part of the new company, he realized that he never again wanted to have his own company, nor did he aspire to head the one he was in. As the company's chief technologist, he was more content than he had ever been.

The large company was enormously challenging to Malcolm, and he delighted in finding ways to improve the company's existing products, as well as coming up with ideas for new ones. He also enjoyed coaching other people through their technological problems. Because he was so knowledgeable and innovative and so quickly contributed to the business, the company gave Malcolm free rein to create his job description. He told them he didn't want to supervise people, and he wanted to report to the CEO. Malcolm also said that he would like to attend every one of his son's football games; he served as the team's assistant coach. Certainly, Malcolm could have demanded more from his organization, and his acumen made him a potential candidate to succeed the CEO. Instead, Malcolm recognized that he had everything he wanted in his current job, and he was clear with both himself and others that this was the case.

Gradually Losing Focus: Marissa

Contrast Malcolm with Marissa, who had done consistently well in marketing positions over the course of a thirty-year career. She had always brought a good mixture of marketing savvy and managerial skill to these positions, and on top of that she was empathic and trusted by her direct reports. We were called in to coach Marissa, though, because in her most recent position as vice president of marketing for a major airline, she was struggling. Given the intense competition and financial uncertainties, potential bankruptcies, and price wars all airlines have been going through, the position was a challenge. Marissa, however, seemed ideally suited to the job and, given her history, it was surprising that she wasn't doing better.

The information we were given suggested that she seemed to have lost her focus. Direct reports complained that Marissa wasn't available to them, didn't offer clear directions, and wasn't willing to take the time to provide them with much useful feedback. What was confusing to both direct reports and her supervisor was that, at times, Marissa was her old self; she still worked well with the company's outside advertising and public relations agencies and provided them with strong direction. In other instances, Marissa did not seem to be a strong leader, have a clear vision, or bring as much energy to this senior role as it required.

If you weren't aware of what the passages entail, you might think that Marissa was in a slump, either dealing with a personal issue or just being unable to function well at the top. In reality, she was going through the letting-go-of-ambition passage. She eventually told us that she had promised herself that she would work for the airline for five years and then retire (she had been with them for two years when we started working with her). Though she was pleased with her retirement timeframe, she was finding it difficult to come to terms with her new persona.

As a female marketing executive who had encountered bias because of her gender, she had always fought hard for her promotions. Marissa had put in a great deal of time and effort to master organizational politics and had made a number of savvy career moves. For the first time, however, she had no desire to be political. She wasn't scanning the organization or the outside for better opportunities, or competing in meetings, or trying to influence her boss to obtain more real estate or treasure. As much as she liked her current job and was perfectly content to do it for the next three years, she was unconsciously reducing her impact because she was oblivious to this passage. Marissa had assumed that her ambition was the reason she worked so hard and so well. Having let go of her ambition, she had lost some of her energy and vitality. Only when she became aware of this letting-go process and talked about it was she able to focus on something else of importance—doing outstanding work, developing people, and leaving a legacy. She realized that she had a great job, that she liked the company and the industry and needed to direct her considerable talent to doing the job as well as she possibly could. She was entering the "mastery" stage of her career, in which constant progression is replaced by constant improvement.

How to Navigate the Passage Successfully

Let's look at how you can avoid Marissa's problems with this passage and take advantage of how Malcolm navigated his way through it.

Like the previous two passages, this one is highly personal because it requires you to come to terms with who you are. It is impossible to navigate this passage successfully unless you grapple with what drives you and how this drive may have changed over the years. At first, you may be anxious about what you discover. In our society and especially in business, ambition is deified. To acknowledge that you no longer are striving for a better-paying job or more prestigious title may seem heretical. In reality, it can be a liberating experience that will make you a more effective leader.

To let go of ambition and replace it in a positive way, do the following:

• *Accept that eventually this happens to everyone, and now it has happened to you.* Years ago, psychologist David McClelland identified three basic motivational patterns: affiliation, achievement, and power. It is not unusual for affiliation to be the dominant motivator of teenage years, with achievement becoming more important during the years of career advancement. But as McClelland found, for almost everyone the desire to achieve reaches a peak, and other motivations in life then become dominant. It is a passage that almost everyone goes through, but what makes this one unique is that it often occurs long before formal retirement begins. Though they probably aren't talking about it, many senior executives have let go of ambition. In a way, they've recognized that they work within a pyramid and there's only room for one at the top. They no longer have to strive and strain to get their shot at the top job, and this gives them a kind of power they never had before.

Acceptance is more than a passive realization that you're content where you are. With this realization comes fear ("I've lost my drive") and lethargy ("Why should I work hard?"). Talking to a trusted coach or mentor about these issues will help you move past them. A good adviser can put your experience in context, demonstrating that letting go of ambition is a lesson all leaders need to learn sooner or later. Giving up is the sign of a still-ambitious leader who has failed and can't handle the failure.

• *Redirect your energy.* If you think about it, you'll realize that the total amount of time you spend networking, schmoozing bosses, and interviewing for jobs can be days or even weeks over the course of a year. Just as significant, you invest a great deal of emotional energy in this quest, spending sleepless nights worrying about the opportunity you missed or sweating out a selection process. As an exercise, do the following:

- Estimate the number of hours you've spent during the past ten years lobbying your boss for advancement, working for visibility in the organization, seeking to obtain credit for your contributions, elbowing aggressive peers out of the way, or even talking to headhunters and consultants about other opportunities.

- Create a list of jobs that you've dreamed about having but never obtained and a list of jobs you were considered for but not selected.

- Think about whether your work performance was adversely affected because of the stress and anxiety of competition— pushing for more, jockeying for position, or trying to move up. Is it possible your performance has been affected?

If you're like most people, this exercise will help you realize that you now have an additional amount of emotional energy and time that you can use to increase your effectiveness in any way you choose. Think about your current job and how it gives you the most satisfaction. What would you like to spend more time doing? What can you focus on that might significantly help your people or the organization as a whole? Is there a particular pet project that you've always wanted to tackle? These types of questions will help you determine how you can ratchet up your effectiveness when going through this passage.

• *Redefine achievement.* Many executives confuse ambition and achievement. They measure their success in dollars earned, titles gained, and key positions assigned. At a certain point in a career, these measurements have validity. During this particular passage, however, new measures must be created. Perhaps you start measuring achievement based on time spent doing your favorite work activity. Perhaps you measure it based on progress toward a goal you value, such as revenue booked, growth in profitability, market cap, market position, new products introduced, lawsuits won, or any other metric. Remember, too, that just because you have let go of ambition doesn't mean you have let go of ambitious projects. Now, though, the project is not a means to an end.

A Legacy of Service to Others

Leaders who let go of ambition are an organization's wise men and women. Having become clearer about their own purpose in life, they are dedicated to the work itself rather than their own careers. As a result, they often receive tremendous respect from direct reports and other colleagues who know they're not operating with personal agendas. People seek them out for advice and support.

Leaders who transcend ambition have the opportunity to become truly expert in their areas of interest. Free of career imperatives, they can devote themselves to what they do best. As a result, they become the organization's experts in given areas, the way Malcolm was his company's technology guru. Not only do they have more time and energy to gather information but they no longer worry about the political implications of pursuing projects that won't further their careers. They are willing to risk failure in order to gain important knowledge.

Recently, we encountered a senior executive who had participated in an executive program several years before, and we were amazed at his personal transformation. He had lost weight, was exercising regularly and eating right, and seemed relaxed and happy. He was still employed as a senior leader in a large global company, so when we asked about the cause for his transformation, he said "retention agreement." What he meant was that due to a merger, he had signed a contract promising to stay with his company for three years, after which time he would receive a significant bonus. Because of this agreement, his usual competitive nature was tamed. He now knew what he would be doing and where he would be working for the immediate future. Suddenly, he became more calm, focused, and relaxed. At this moment, he was focused on achievement in a healthier way, including taking better care of himself. He was less driven but more grounded as a leader, and probably more productive.

It shouldn't come as a surprise that leaders who have let go of ambition are usually a company's best developers of talent. Developing other people is sometimes difficult for those who are working hard on their own careers. They may see their direct reports as competition for jobs to which they aspire. More commonly, they prefer devoting their time and energy to helping themselves succeed rather than helping others. Despite all the talk about the need to develop talent, leaders often feel that the rewards for doing so are less than achieving other goals.

A few years ago, Honeywell International instituted an award for the company's best people developers, worldwide. Thousands of dollars and much recognition were given annually to about fifty winners who were nominated by peers at the local level. The winners were remarkable leaders who, as a group, represented another way to achieve success in a modern company. They left a remarkable legacy of people who had flourished under their leadership—something they will remember far longer than profitability, revenue, projects completed, or meetings attended.

When you let go of ambition, what you frequently gain is satisfaction from the success of others. You have reached a point where you want to pass on your wisdom to a future generation. Rather than guard your knowledge and use it to advance, you want other people to gain from your expertise. When you go through this passage successfully, you gain the patience and generosity required of a teacher. In the past, impatient with a direct report's lack of experience, you may have been reluctant to demonstrate, teach, and listen because you had more important matters to attend to. Now demonstrating, teaching, and listening have more priority.

When an organization's senior leadership team is composed only of people who are striving to get ahead, the culture reflects that competition at the top. Although competition drives capitalism and is important in business, so is the development of people, and many companies are fortunate to have wise men and women at the top who have let go of the ambition to move ahead; they embody the best of the culture. Someone has to develop the leaders of tomorrow. Someone has to focus on finding ways of doing the work more effectively. When you let go of your ambition, you add a valuable element to your company's leadership mix.

14

Facing Personal Upheaval

Under the broad heading of "personal upheaval," we find a wide range of disasters, crises, and pain. Most common are the death of a loved one, physical illness or disability, and divorce. Also included might be problems with children (especially adolescents), legal difficulties, and financial struggles. Though the substance of each of these problems might be different, all create chaos in leaders' lives. Uncertainty becomes prevalent, both in terms of functioning and feeling. Nothing is the same as it was before the upheaval.

Most people don't think of these events as having anything to do with leadership. Most executives categorize death, divorce, or grief as private matters. They speak of them among their executive peers only to announce that they've split with their spouse or that they won't be in for a few days because a loved one has died. Beyond announcing the fact of the personal difficulty, though, many leaders rarely share their feelings about what has occurred and how it is creating upheaval. To do so would seem like a sign of weakness in a corporate world that defines *professionalism* as the absence of any emotion, a world of work in which life's ups and downs are somehow not relevant to performance. What's more, as the world seems increasingly politically correct, some people even deem it inappropriate or dangerous to inquire after the personal well-being of another. Many older executives grew up in corporations where bosses adopted a tough, militaristic persona. Even younger executives, both men and women, sometimes refuse to allow their personal dilemmas and tragedies to intrude into the office, lest they appear weak or out of control. Such an obsessively businesslike demeanor stifles leadership development.

Most leaders interviewed for this book cited the passage of personal loss or upheaval as a significant turning point in their development, both individually and professionally. Still, despite the fact that, invariably, it seems unproductive to talk about personal matters at work, they are in the long run what create a truly human leader. The worst possible reaction to personal upheaval is denying to yourself or others that anything is wrong, behaving in the same way as you always have, or covering up the actuality of what you are experiencing. Not only does an inauthentic approach distance others, your unnatural stoicism will undermine trust—the basis of great leadership. Human relationships exist on both a verbal and nonverbal level, and the nonverbal information frequently carries more impact than what is spoken. The lack of congruence between words and demeanor may create credibility issues, especially for those who do not know what you are experiencing. Denial also prevents you from moving on and growing as a result of this personal difficulty.

How Tragedy Affects Direction

We'd like to share a few powerful stories of people who have dealt with their personal upheavals in different ways.

Humanization of a Leader: Jim

Jim Renier was the CEO and chairman of Honeywell in the nineties. Before reaching the top of Honeywell, Jim was a hard-driving executive with a reputation for forming competitive relationships with others in order to achieve his goals. With a doctorate in chemical

The biggest setback I ever had in my life was my divorce
from my first wife. That was a big one. It was not only that,
it was that I was then separated from my three very young
children. I was just getting going and building some assets,
and they were all stripped away. At the end of that process,
I was divorced; I had lost all my assets and I was living in
a rooming house. I still had my job, and my children were
living about an hour away. I was still in a formative part of
my career. I had no money for a house or anything. I would
visit my children every weekend, and there was no place
to go because I didn't have a home. That was my situation,
and I went through a whole process of "What am I trying
to do? Where am I going? What is important? What is not
important? How am I going to behave?" All of that, as
well as examining what the aspects of myself were that
contributed to the situation. It had to do with, "What is
my attitude and my attitude toward my ex-wife? What am
I trying to do with the three children I have? What am I
trying to do with my career? Where does it all fit together?"
I would say of all the things in my life, that was the fork in
the road. It could have gone in a very different direction.
I spent six years on my own. I didn't just quickly look for
a wife; a lot of people make mistakes that way. I think
Socrates said it all. He said, "Know thyself." Until you
really know yourself, you can never reach down and grab
all the strength that's within you. You have to know who
you are. The things that differentiate you, the things
that make you strong and good, the things that are your
shortcomings that will probably never change.

RAY VIAULT, VICE CHAIRMAN, GENERAL MILLS

engineering and the scientific mind to match, as well as a strong personality and a highly aggressive leadership style, Jim was not always a warm-and-fuzzy leader who was beloved by his employees. He was smart, strategic, and great at getting results, though, and this kept him moving forward.

As he was rising through the ranks of Honeywell, Jim's wife became ill with cancer. He spent a great deal of time taking care of her, as well as their young children. Then she died, and Jim eventually returned to work but not as the same type of person and leader he had been. The entire process of nursing his wife, grieving for her when she died, and then helping his children come to terms with their loss and raising them as a single parent was no doubt emotionally difficult for Jim. He was placed in a situation in which he had to act differently from the way he ever had before and had to confront intense feelings.

When he returned to work, by his own report Jim became a changed man. The experience had humanized him. He was more in touch with his feelings and was much more empathic and compassionate than he had been before. Jim became a different kind of leader—a scientist interested in human relationships. He launched a program at Honeywell designed to help other results-driven engineering leaders understand the importance of self-esteem. Jim also talked about this passage in a very public way, helping people understand how the issues he confronted ultimately changed him as a person and as a leader, giving him the emotional maturity necessary to be selected as chairman of Honeywell and be an effective leader of the company.

Regression as a Leader: Drew

Unlike Jim, Drew was an empathetic leader from the start. He worked his way up to the top HR position in his corporation, in part because he was an excellent administrator but also because he did a great job of supporting the development of talent within the company. Drew's team enjoyed working with him and felt that he was a supportive and caring boss.

Drew was happily married with three children. The middle son was an athlete—a football player who tested limits. Drew had tried to set limits, but his son generally ignored them, and Drew was not a strict disciplinarian. One night, Drew's son left a party drunk and drove his car into a tree. He survived the accident but his back was broken, leaving him paralyzed from the neck down. Drew blamed himself for the accident. He plunged into a deep depression, berating himself for failing to be more strict and more effective as a parent in communicating to his son the dangers of drinking and driving.

Two days after the accident, Drew returned to work. Though everyone knew what had happened, he declined to share any information other than to say his son had been injured in a car accident and was still in the hospital. He resisted his manager's entreaties to find out about what he was experiencing or might need. Drew insisted that work was the best therapy, and he began spending long hours at the office. It was almost as if he felt he could submerge his guilt in work.

As a consequence of his son's paralysis, Drew's behaviors changed, not necessarily in an overtly negative way. He began to emphasize details—a reasonable trait in an HR department head. But so much of his time and attention were focused on little things that some big things were ignored. For instance, he fell far behind schedule on a critical project—a revamp of hiring protocols designed to meet new legal requirements—because he was focused on a new software implementation. Though Drew remained approachable and empathetic, everyone noted that his empathy seemed more perfunctory than heartfelt. He'd listen, nod, and express the right sentiments, but he always seemed distracted.

After two years, the company demoted Drew. It wasn't that he had become a poor leader. He had simply regressed. The HR department was not functioning as smoothly or as innovatively as it had in the past, and Drew did not appear to be engaged.

Drew regressed as a leader, not because of the tragedy in his life alone but because he was unable to grieve his loss, confront his guilt, and move on. It's impossible to know whether Drew would have been able to rebound from his loss had he accepted his manager's offer of help, had he been more open with his team and himself about his feelings. The odds are that adversity provided an opening for him to know himself better. Alas, either because of his background, beliefs, or behavior, he could not summon the resolve to actually accomplish this.

Transformation as a Leader: Guiliani

Consider a third leader who was transformed by tragedy: Rudolph Guiliani. Before 9/11, some people viewed New York's mayor as arrogant and abrasive. After 9/11, his image changed because of how he responded to the terrorist attack and the loss of so many people. He didn't respond with fist-shaking threats against the terrorists or the studied calm of someone playing the role of leader. Instead, he shared his grief with the openness of an ordinary human being, and he made himself available to those who needed consolation, inspiration, and hope. Nothing he said or did seemed scripted. He was real, emotional, and thoughtful. Because he allowed his true nature to emerge in this difficult time, he became an incredibly powerful and effective leader. His vulnerability created a bond with millions of others who shared his grief, sense of loss, and humanity and demonstrated what effective leadership really should be.

How to Manage Upheaval

Whatever form your personal upheaval takes, your feelings are a catalyst to make you a better leader. This is easy to write but difficult to put into practice, especially for men. Many women tend to do a better job being open with their emotions, acknowledging their upset from a divorce or their fury because of the way their child is behaving. Women often seek out a colleague at work (usually another woman) with whom to process their experience. Men tend to focus more on goals and on fixing things rather than experiencing or expressing their feelings, so this passage presents special challenges. We've coached many executives who admit they have talked themselves into believing that they were functioning acceptably during a personal crisis, when in fact they were distracted and working at half-speed. The fact is, you're most likely to make major work mistakes when you give the appearance of being fine while inside you're anything but. Others assume you have recovered from your problems. Sometimes, in an effort to distract or help you, they give you the usual tasks, new responsibilities, or challenges. At such a time, you are ill-equipped to handle them.

To learn and grow during a difficult time in your life and to use adversity for leadership development, consider doing the following:

• *Reveal your vulnerabilities*. Grief is a common, human experience. It binds us all. No one is expert at handling grief or hardship, and yet we all feel that we should be better at doing so. Leadership, in fact, may be viewed as providing a model and permission to others for how to handle this universal, difficult, inescapable human experience. As counterintuitive as it might seem, explaining your struggle to others, coming to terms with an adverse medical diagnosis, dealing with difficult children, and working through loss humanizes you as a leader and actually makes you more, not less, effective. Asking for additional support from others during a difficult passage is not weakness but strength. Our reluctance to show our vulnerability invokes our fear of appearing weak. In reality, being vulnerable humanizes us, connects us to others, and empowers rather than weakens us as leaders. Direct reports want their leaders to be human; they already know they have weaknesses as well as strengths; disguising them creates distance that affects performance. Followers appreciate tough-but-tender leaders: tough in demanding performance, tender in their ability to understand and appreciate our humanity. Leaders, too, respect those who are courageous enough to be open about their dilemmas and feelings and open as well about what they can and cannot handle.

• *Be authentic.* There is a temptation to play a role in order to get through this passage. You become the "Strong, Courageous Leader" or the "Inwardly Suffering, Outwardly Cheerful Boss" because that is the role you believe others will accept, even prefer. In reality, you appear to be distanced from yourself and ungrounded, which may actually cause others to avoid or distrust you. If you tell everyone you're okay but isolate yourself in your office, others may provide support by avoiding you, believing you don't want to see or talk to them. The effort to be genuine is important. Obviously, you don't want to arrive every day at work in tears or require others to endure lengthy discussion of your pain. What you can do is allow your sadness or anger to surface under the right circumstances—for example, when you are talking to trusted others and have the time and privacy with which to engage in this type of conversation.

• *Accept fate and move on.* The people who handle this passage best are able to accept that life is uncertain and frequently painful, and they can accept this without bitterness. Nor do they drown in guilt. They reflect instead on what has happened and, after a period of time, make peace with it.

You've probably known colleagues or friends who can't move past a personal upheaval. They are the ones who remain stuck in a painful transition. They recover from an illness but remain filled with self-pity. We're suggesting that you find a way to come to terms with whatever negative event has taken place as a catalyst for both personal growth and leadership development. Adversity creates leadership strength. Finding a way to grow may require taking any number of paths—meditation perhaps, or prayer, therapy, reflection, or sabbatical. Even committing to a larger purpose or cause in order to create meaning can restore order to your life and help you emerge from the confusing aspects of the event. Once you've done this, you can determine what you want to do next in the sense of setting new goals and doing what's needed to achieve them.

How Fresh Perspective Brings Leadership Maturity

In some ways, you can't be a truly mature, wise leader until you go through this passage successfully. Until you've grappled with the death of a loved one, an illness, a child who takes the wrong path, or a divorce, you've enjoyed a life free of major, personal pain. Personal upheaval humanizes leaders and enhances their ability to connect with other people.

Think about how Jim Ranier, Rudy Guiliani, and countless other leaders were humanized by this passage. They grew wiser and more empathic by revealing their vulnerabilities, being authentic, accepting fate, and moving on.

Remember, though, that experiencing personal upheaval won't automatically transform you into a wise, empathetic leader. Consider how some people go through a divorce. You've probably known a colleague who has been through a difficult divorce, and even if you didn't know the spouse, you may have suspected a few reasons the relationship didn't work out. Both before and after the divorce, he treats his direct reports without respect. No doubt this attitude affected other relationships as well, probably his primary one. Some people, however, recognize that the behaviors that produced the divorce are also ones that harm workplace relationships. They comprehend that they can use the lessons of their divorce to create

When I was in the rooming house and I had no assets and my children were elsewhere and there was no possibility of reconciliation, it was so easy to feel sorry for myself and to go into a spiral. I think . . . . it's the life-changing experiences to which you also contribute, like the divorce situation, that are really fundamental in shaping you. I've felt like I've been under pressure at various times, but I've always felt that I knew who I was and what I was trying to do. If people didn't want that, I always had the confidence that, well, I'll just move on and I'll find some other situation rather than allowing other people to control my emotions.

RAY VIAULT, VICE CHAIRMAN, GENERAL MILLS

sustainable human connections in all areas of their lives. As a result, they become more human in the best sense of that word.

Death, too, is a harsh but effective teacher. We transcend our grief, anger, and guilt by paying attention to what our emotions are telling us. Some highly energetic, demanding leaders unconsciously deny the possibility of their own deaths. They drive themselves and others mercilessly, neglecting their families and earning reputations as difficult and unpleasant bosses. The death of someone they love, however, offers them renewal—a second chance at being a more understanding person and a better leader. When they accept that death is something they can't overcome with achievement, power, or money, they moderate their driving, controlling behaviors. They return from a period of mourning with a new outlook on everything in their lives, and this fresh perspective translates into leadership maturity. As the Buddhists say, "If you want to understand your life, practice your death," which is to say, acknowledging that life is finite enriches it with meaning.

When Companies Don't Help

Companies are rational systems. They value logic, and their tight structures and rigid policies provide a bulwark against the messy aspects of human behavior and the unpredictable hand of fate. Given the rational foundation of organizations, grief, rage, and other extreme emotional states are anathema. Who knows what mistake a grief-stricken executive in charge of the manufacturing process might make? Who knows what a rage-filled manager might say to his boss if he doesn't like what his boss tells him to do?

For this reason, organizations attempt to compartmentalize grief and other strong emotions. They provide coaching for executives who are being difficult, conflict resolution sessions to deal with angry arguments, time off for those who are grieving, and medical benefits for people who need therapy. All this is fine, but strong emotions can't be effectively compartmentalized. People may decide to tuck their emotional outbursts back inside after being talked to, but the emotions remain, especially after some form of personal upheaval.

A better way for companies to handle the deaths and divorces that happen in most executives' lives is to foster a culture similar to the one that exists in high-performing teams. A hallmark of these teams is emotional and intellectual honesty. People are given the license to be real. Under intense pressure and with highly ambitious objectives, these teams can't function without each member saying exactly how he feels. They don't have the luxury to posture, play politics, or avoid stepping on toes.

In emotionally honest cultures, individuals are empowered to speak from the heart. They get their hurts out in the open, and this gives the group an opportunity to participate in the healing of these hurts. Personal upheaval is never easy to deal with, especially if the loss of a loved one is involved, but enlightened companies are gradually learning to help their leaders grow from the experience rather than allow them to self-destruct.

15

Losing Faith in the System

In an era of corporate scandal, CEO indictments, and accounting crimes, losing faith in the system is a passage that reflects the time in which we live. If you talk to associates and employees in most large companies today, and they are candid (as they tend to be during leadership development programs), you will quickly discern a higher degree of skepticism, even cynicism. Not only are they cynical and skeptical about the business world in general but they feel that way about their organization and its leaders, specifically. At some point, these individuals cross the line from uncertainty to a lack of faith, and at this point they are in a predictable, intense passage.

We've listened to many senior leaders talk about their companies and about why they've lost faith in the system, and we have heard something along the following lines:

> I've worked seventeen years for this company in a variety of roles and made a huge commitment to the organization. I've traveled, relocated, worked weekends, cut short or cancelled vacations. I made a commitment to this company because I believed in what it stood for. Now I wonder whether what it says it stands for and what it really is all about are two different things.

People who lose faith feel betrayed for reasons that can vary from witnessing a single unethical act to enduring a whole series of disillusioning events. The CEO may have communicated one course of action and then reversed course. The *Wall Street Journal* may have reported an SEC investigation, or the FDA may be undertaking a regulatory action. It may be that senior leaders announced that acquisitions have been ruled out as a growth strategy, only to have a large acquisition announced several months later.

It is also possible that the sense of betrayal is the result of a relationship-driven promotion system. Or perhaps promotions are politically based rather than based on obvious merit. People can also lose faith because of the way individuals are treated. An accumulation of personal upsets may include such incidents as the easing out of an executive with long service shortly before she is eligible for retirement or the abrupt termination of an employee who has received nothing but glowing performance reviews throughout his career. Less than honest communication to avoid litigation can also create wariness and cynicism about those who convey ambiguous messages.

In all these cases, a disconnect appears between how people want to perceive their companies and how they actually experience them. They assume them to be ethical but continually observe examples in which senior leaders use data to support preconceived decisions. Or they learn about their CEO's pay package while working on his assignment to implement rigid cost controls throughout the company. People lose faith in the system when management doesn't practice organizational values, or top leaders are seen to act in ways they themselves would not.

Losing Faith and Finding Meaning

When you lose faith, you mortgage your commitment as a leader. But as we'll see, you have the option of developing your leadership capabilities, even when your faith has disappeared.

Overcoming Disillusionment

When Lisa interviewed and was selected for a midlevel legal position at a Silicon Valley company, she was pleased. She had previously worked in the Midwest as assistant general counsel for a family-run business, and though she liked the owners, she never felt particularly comfortable there. Lisa was very liberal in her politics and social views, but she felt that the founder and owner of the company was a staunch conservative whose politics translated into a poor record on minority hiring and who was willing to support only charitable causes that reinforced his own political viewpoint. She stayed there five years, enjoyed her work, and was well rewarded, but when she heard about an opening at the Silicon Valley company—a company that regularly received glowing notices in the media for being a great place for women to work—she applied for and got the job.

Lisa's first four years with the company were successful. Not only was she promoted twice but the company put her on the advisory group of two ongoing, highly visible philanthropic programs. During this time, Lisa truly believed she was working for the best organization in the country and told this to her family and friends, as well as to new hires she was recruiting. She admired the CEO's decisions and communication, and felt the company's culture and values were ideally suited to her beliefs and work style.

With her second promotion to general counsel, Lisa joined the CEO's team of direct reports. Shortly afterward, she began to view the company differently; she began to lose faith. Coincidentally, the dot-com bubble of the late nineties was beginning to implode, and the company's stock began to fall. Among several difficult moves, the company decided to cut funding to several worthy causes, including a breast cancer research center. During an advisory committee meeting on the company's foundation donations, the CEO and two male direct reports made a joke that when the economy rebounded, they would have to find another women's disease they could support. "Let's look at ovaries next time," one of the executives said.

Everyone laughed, and though Lisa didn't say anything, she noted their insensitivity and boorish behavior. Later, she participated in another difficult meeting in which the CEO and his direct reports discussed head-count reduction. As part of the discussion, they focused on the external message to accompany their decisions. The strategy was to cut deeply into full-time employment in order to convince Wall Street analysts and reporters that the company was serious about cost control. The CEO commented that he wanted to position the company as "more fiscally responsible than the Street gives us credit for." Lisa's position was that there might be other alternatives than terminating numerous talented and skilled employees. The CEO suggested that Lisa, because of her newness to the management committee, might not be experienced in managing through a down business cycle.

Lisa was astonished that her idealism about the CEO and his management team could have been so inaccurate. But sitting in on management meetings, in combination with the economic downturn, fueled her new perception that her colleagues' values were situational and opportunistic. The top managers fostered the positive appearance of leading a "good place to work," but it was an illusion. They did not walk their talk.

For a while, Lisa struggled with her new perceptions. Initially, she was angry with the CEO and his team and seriously considered quitting. The more she thought about this alternative, though, the less attractive it seemed. She loved her job, the rewards that came with it, and being part of the Silicon Valley high-tech culture. More significantly, she realized that even though she was less enthusiastic about her company's leadership, she still relished working with many of the company's bright people, especially her own team. She took great pride in having developed her direct reports, and she didn't want to desert them. In addition, Lisa still represented her company on the board of a national environmental group, and she knew that if she were to leave the company, she would need to relinquish that role. Lisa realized that despite her anger and disillusionment, she had a meaningful job and could continue to feel good about herself as a person and as a leader if she remained with the company.

Making Good Choices

Instinctively, Lisa made the right choices as she began looking at her company critically. She could have reacted by resigning. Or she could have stayed but grown increasingly cynical, getting stuck in this passage because she couldn't forgive the CEO for being a different leader from the one she had thought him to be. She found a way to re-energize herself instead.

Here are some dos and don'ts that will help you when you find yourself in a similar passage. First the don'ts:

• *Don't seek refuge in cynicism.* To Lisa's credit, she bypassed the cynical stage. Many are not so fortunate. Cynicism appears with great regularity to leaders when their initial idealism is dispelled. Typically, young leaders join organizations fresh from other companies or assignments and are excited and energized about work. If they're lucky, they eventually find a challenging role with a good boss, working for a company with an outstanding reputation that offers them the opportunity to do things they've always wanted to do, as well as to learn and grow. Over time, however, idealistic new people inevitably lose some of their excitement and energy. They may have a boss who, in recruiting them, promises an opportunity that never materializes. They realize that the excitement of corporate travel requires them to sacrifice time with friends or the opportunity to build satisfying relationships. They learn that senior managers, who have a great impact on the organizational culture, are also flawed human beings. They discover that the organization they thought they were working for was only imaginary; the real one doesn't fulfill their expectations.

In most companies, as we have observed, over time people form a scar of cynicism to cover up their wounded ideals. We encounter many cynical people today who make fun of their organizational culture, subtly criticize decisions, convey skepticism that things will ever change, and disparage other leaders as ways of coping with their disillusionment. In many instances, these critical leaders bond with others who share a similar outlook, engaging in conversations whose sole purpose is to mock institutional policies and senior managers' actions.

The result: leaders who work without purpose. They do their jobs efficiently and effectively but without real commitment, just going through the motions. They lack passion and energy. They are unwilling to do anything extra or to take any real risks that put themselves on the edge. There is no better way to limit your own development as a leader than by seeking refuge in cynicism.

Unfortunately, this strategy also makes their existence less productive. If your focus is on escape, you can't be stretching yourself or your team, or taking on new and diverse experiences, or putting yourself at risk. When you believe your company is impossible to change, escape fantasies salve your wounded idealism. The problem, of course, is that they don't make you into a more effective leader.

• *Don't be a victim.* When you stop believing in the organization, you may feel like a victim. You're convinced that the company or the entire world has misled you, and now you have to pay the price. You go around the office or your home bemoaning your fate and the dastardly bosses who led you astray.

Self-pity is neither pretty nor productive. Although your feelings of hurt and anger are legitimate, they do not supply permission to feel powerless. If you've ever worked with a victim, you know how enervating it is. People lose faith when they give up. Their pessimism and resignation suck the life out of teams.

You may well have been victimized by an unethical leader in your organization or a company that has blundered into serious missteps, but whether you play the victim is your choice. We coach senior leaders on a maxim of leadership: *it is impossible to be an executive victim.* That is to say, when you choose to be a leader and when many people are counting on you and your competence, you are not a victim of anyone else's power. In most companies, you can regain your power to influence other people and achieve goals, and if you recognize this fact, you won't act or think like a victim.

Now, on the positive side, here is what you can do.

• *Create meaningful work for yourself.* Even in a worst-case scenario—your company is under investigation, predicted to fall into bankruptcy, or in some serious downward spiral—you can still find purpose when you grasp that meaningful work may be different from the way you conceived it. Some leaders convince themselves that winning is what is meaningful about their job or that work is all about a particular title, salary, boss, or company. When they lose faith in these systemic elements, they feel betrayed. They thought that working for a great boss or great company was what work was all about, and now that they know it is not, what's left?

What's left is the meaning you create for yourself. Here are the three ways leaders renew faith in their jobs, their careers, and their leadership roles:

1. *Through other people.* You are responsible for your direct reports. They look to you for guidance; they expect you to help develop them. Take this responsibility seriously. Focus on the reality that other people's work lives are in your hands and that if you lose faith and sink into cynicism or victimhood, you'll be worthless to them. You may also find meaning in helping a boss achieve goals. You may be disillusioned by the CEO's actions, but you still respect your boss. If you believe in what he is trying to accomplish, focus your effort on making his goal your goal.

2. *Through a specific project on which you're working.* Just because you believe the organizational system is bankrupt doesn't mean it taints everything it touches. You can find meaning in specific tasks. Your next project assignment may be worthwhile, whether it's developing a new manufacturing process or creating knowledge networks. The work itself can be fulfilling if you work diligently and creatively.

3. *Through your sense of achievement.* Even within a moral vacuum, achievement is possible. You can learn new skills, create provocative ideas, and even inject good values into a corrupt system. In other words, you can achieve a lot in any leadership position, and the feeling of achievement will help sustain you, even if you no longer believe in the company or its leaders.

• *Reconnect with what originally drew you to your area of expertise or the business world in general.* Some people lose faith in the system, not because of any specific act of malfeasance on the part of senior management but because they've grown jaded. Maybe their careers haven't worked out exactly as they had planned or they had impossibly high expectations that could never be met.

We've found that veteran executives can find new meaning by refocusing on what initially excited them about their business. Sometimes they recall one of the passages we've discussed, such as their first stretch assignment or being in charge of a business for the first time. Whatever it is, the focus on replicating their initial excitement can help to replace what is now missing. To recapture their purpose, they may simply need to request another stretch assignment. We've coached senior vice presidents in the later stages of their careers who have volunteered to work in their company's office in an undeveloped country, because they relished living and working in another culture and enjoyed the challenge of living with risk. Some executives recall their first mentor with gratitude, and they want to pay back the system by mentoring others. All of this can help rekindle your drive and sense of purpose.

Purposeful Leadership

Certainly there are leaders—senior executives included—who are cynical, manipulative, and political and who destroy the faith of others in the company and business. In our experience, despite what the media present, the vast majority don't fit this profile. In most cases, people selected for top positions are driven, committed, and competent, and they believe in what they're doing.

In this passage, you learn the importance of a sense of purpose. Up until this point, you may have worked hard and effectively, but you never really came to terms with why you do what you do. Losing faith in the system challenges you to discover your rationale for work. You learn that when you have an internal reason for leading others and accomplishing goals, you derive great satisfaction from your job. You stop relying on the company, your boss, or even your financial obligations to provide you with external motivation and instead summon it from within yourself.

Most of the great leaders we've worked with have this capacity. Whether or not they lost faith in the system, they have great faith in their own personal reasons for coming to work each day and doing the best they can. You can spot a leader with a sense of purpose from a distance, and so can other executives evaluating candidates for promotion to senior positions. The paradox of this passage is that losing faith in the system helps you gain a greater belief in yourself.

16

How Companies Can Use Passages to Develop Leadership

Up to now, we've focused on ways individuals can navigate these predictable, intense passages to become more effective leaders. Although we've noted ways organizations can facilitate these passages (and how they sometimes fail to do so), we recognize that many companies are eager to use this material on a broader scale. Most companies today use succession-planning systems and talent reviews to develop leaders. Since the early work of Lombardo and McCall, we have also known about the importance of experiences in leadership development, even though most of the work done in this area has focused on positive, definable, even measurable, career experiences and events.

In this book, we have looked at experiences in a broader sense. Now we'd like to offer some ways you can implement a leadership passage strategy on a larger scale. Let's take a one-chapter break from the focus on the individual and see how the organization itself can participate more effectively in the leadership development process.

Traditional Leadership Development

Companies are aware of leadership transitions. Most corporate leaders today know about Daniel Goleman's work on emotional intelligence and his premise that intelligence alone is insufficient for success in interdependent teams and organizations. Goleman also points out that self-awareness, self-regulation, and the understanding of how to self-motivate are key components of emotional intelligence. Today many companies offer coaching to leaders to improve their interpersonal skills and relationships, especially those who may be technically competent but less effective communicating with and motivating peers and direct reports.

What companies generally don't do, however, is integrate Goleman's insights about emotional intelligence, including the factors around self-awareness and self-regulation, into the core "people processes" of selection, assessment, promotion, and development. When a leader is identified as technically competent but in need of behavioral change, she is often assigned a coach who is asked to work confidentially with the executive; the underlying issues are deemed too complicated, messy, or private to be part of the business conversation.

We have observed that in many companies today, leadership development tends to be managed in a fairly narrow way. Attributes of leadership are identified, usually based on performance competencies of current high-visibility leaders. Leadership development aimed at this target is then undertaken in a classroom-oriented, skill-based, strictly cognitive environment.

The critical leadership passages described in this book—transitions faced by every successful executive—tend to be seen as peripheral to core people processes rather than integral to them. Most organizations are concerned with how they can prepare someone for the next job. The key focus is, "What does this person already know and what do we need to teach him?" rather than, "What does this *particular* individual need to understand?" When experience and competency dominate who is hired, promoted, and developed, individuals who become leaders are often strong performers but not always strong leaders.

For example, you may be very good at sales, manufacturing, or finance, or have succeeded at a series of positions, but still lack the empathy, wisdom, and maturity required of leaders. In some cases, you can embody a company's model of leadership competency to the letter and still not be a leader anyone would want to follow.

In many fast-moving, successful companies, strong, successful leaders who fail at some challenge present a real dilemma to the organization. Although, as we have seen, failure is a powerful teacher, it can also throw sand into the gears of succession planning. The paradox is that even though Bob's failure may make Bob a stronger leader, it may also make Bob seem weaker in the eyes of everyone else. Rarely is this issue addressed during succession planning. We don't hear the question: "But what did he really learn from that experience of failing at X?" or "How will she now be more effective because of her failure?" Even more important, since life itself is a leadership development experience, rarely are the life events that shape leaders—divorce, death, living cross-culturally, personal transformation—allowed to enter the politically correct discussions that constitute leadership reviews. Companies act instead as if the personal life of a leader doesn't exist.

As coaches, however, we know it does. In fact, one of the unique privileges of being an executive coach is that we are privy to our clients' struggles with everything from bad bosses to balancing family and work. From our conversations with them, it is clear that a lot is going on inside that directly affects how they perform and develop as leaders. Inside companies, however, most leaders maintain a strict separation of the professional and the personal. To their bosses, peers, and direct reports, they seem fine. Beneath the surface, though, they are going through predictable, intense passages, and their company is often unwilling or unable even to acknowledge their journey, much less support them on it. We've concluded that companies are missing a tremendous opportunity to help individuals take responsibility for their own leadership development.

How Organizations Can Facilitate Learning

How can organizations facilitate leadership learning and growth in the passages? In the sections that follow, we offer four suggestions.

In one sense, I don't know where all my own personal motivation and focus comes from. In another sense, I think I got a lot of it from watching my father go through his life and the extent to which he identified and lived his personal value system. I applied his example to situations, for me as a leader, even before Pacific Gas and Electric company filed for Chapter 11 protection. I knew that moving in and out of bankruptcy was going to require focus on some very simple facts and objectives that we couldn't get away from. My dad's example, even now, with his not being well, has given me a huge amount of strength. I tell the members of my team that every bad day I have here is better than a good day for him right now. The lesson to me was that you can get through all of the things in your life, including your own personal declining health and frailty, by having a sense of mission, purpose, and values. That's what I drew from the way my dad lives his life. That makes it very easy to deal with things that are very tough. I don't ever remember consciously adopting that. I've said to many folks that his life's experience has had an impact on me and has helped me to have a values arrow kind of built in.

BOB GLYNN, CHAIRMAN, CEO, AND PRESIDENT, PG&E CORPORATION

Expand the View of Potential Leaders

Those in charge of core people processes must assess and develop the whole person. This means hiring individuals who have more than the right education, background, or core competencies. Hiring decisions should also factor in the diversity and adversity each candidate has experienced, along with exploring how or whether they have helped him change and grow. Someone who has worked at Dell or Microsoft might very well make an excellent leader, but so would someone who has worked in Africa, volunteered in the inner city, or run a political campaign. Truly astute leaders have already figured this out. As one CEO remarked to us, "If I want to find a global leader, I look for the kid who backpacked around

Europe in his twenties, not necessarily the one who went from his B.A. to an internship at IBM." Similarly, a stronger candidate may not have a string of successes on his résumé, but he may have been through an acquisition, divestiture, late-career change of direction, or even significant failure. (As an example, many smart companies we know recently moved quickly to pick up former Arthur Andersen partners and principals, with the correct view that the implosion of that firm produced even smarter professionals.)

A broader understanding and view of experience will lead companies to ask different questions during the core processes of succession and planning. The goal will be to determine what passages people have been through and what they've learned from these experiences. If they encountered a career roadblock, what did they do about it? Did they think long and hard about the obstacle from many angles and learn from it? Did they rationalize it? Did they spin it? Do they feel their work style or sensitivities contributed to their experience? What did the experience teach them about how not to lead? Answers to questions like these are much more insightful about the whole person than questions such as, "What skills did you learn in your last job that will help you perform well in this one?"

Broadening perspective means recognizing that leadership is about character and values, and about building trust, not just about performing competently (see Figure 16.1). Although it is foolish to declare that results don't matter, it is equally foolish to forget that courageous, empathetic leaders generate results. Of course, companies don't consciously view people from narrow perspectives. For instance, most organizations don't explicitly discriminate against women, yet women are still, despite years of emphasis otherwise, woefully underrepresented in senior leadership positions. It is instructive to note that they are not underrepresented in more junior positions. The problem is that companies have narrowly defined parameters for senior leadership, and one of them is that you can't take a midcareer sabbatical and expect to rise to the top. Of course, this is exactly what many women do who start families. A broader view of leadership would recognize that having children is a passage

Figure 16.1. Leadership Development Is About Experiences.

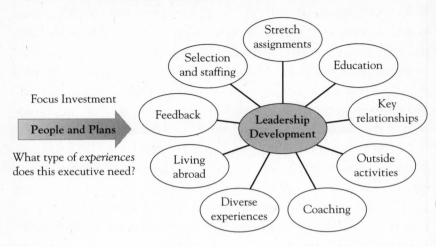

rich in learning and that women can become nurturing, empathetic, and stronger leaders by having children.

Don't Allow Success or Failure to Define Leadership Development

Perhaps the best argument for organizations to heed this advice is what we call the developmental paradox, illustrated by the matrix shown in Figure 16.2.

Figure 16.2. The Developmental Paradox.

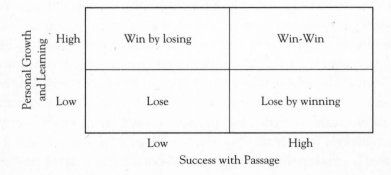

As the matrix suggests, some people may be outwardly successful in a given passage but still end up "losing" because they learned little or nothing from the experience. An individual may go through the passage of joining a company or moving into a leadership role with great success. He performed skillfully in that new position, delivering the results the company expected. To all intents and purposes, he was successful. Inside, however, nothing happened. He didn't reflect on the fears, doubts, and pain he experienced as he tackled the assignment; he didn't ask questions of others or try to gain new knowledge to help with unfamiliar tasks; he didn't test new behaviors to see if they would be more effective in his new role. In short, he didn't do much to foster learning or growth. In a leadership assignment down the road, this "not learning how to learn" will not yield further results.

However, the developmental paradox suggests you can fail in a passage yet still experience high learning and growth. If you reflect and question, and probe why you encountered or even created a significant failure, for instance, you might identify an aspect of your leadership style or behavior that needs to be modified. You can, for example, gain insight into what we have termed your derailment behaviors and work to modify them. This recognition will not only increase your awareness next time you are in similar situations, but it will be the catalyst for you to change attitudes and behaviors and become a more effective leader.

We realize there is little margin or room for failure in today's competitive business environment. What many companies don't realize, however, is that by viewing leadership failure in a broader fashion, they increase the odds for future success. In our experience, a common dilemma leaders must grapple with is how to promote talented people into stretch assignments without risking the business. Although it is true that people learn from stretch and risk, the question is, How far can people be pushed? Frequently, our advice is this: as far as possible. Leaders learn from diversity and adversity, failure included. Good developers find a way to orchestrate learning opportunities and harvest the learning that occurs from negative as well as positive circumstances. We invite potential leaders to take risks that may create adverse circumstances and use the adversity to learn about themselves.

In succession planning, performance reviews, and other assessments, it's tempting to make quick judgments about people based on their successes and failures. We've participated in many succession-planning reviews in which a sharp anecdote can derail an entire career. We're not suggesting that anyone should discount performance but that more productive, open-ended conversations will factor in answers to deeper, more probing questions such as these:

> What did this person learn when he succeeded or failed?
>
> How has he changed because of the experience?
>
> What else do we know about this person's life that has contributed to her learning?
>
> Given this experience, what are the areas for future growth?

Make Every Open Position a Leadership Development Opportunity

Currently, companies are focusing on experience as the best developer of people—a recognition that leadership development must take place outside the classroom. If you can match the right person with the right position, you can trigger a passage that greatly accelerates development. Many companies simply give people jobs and let them sink or swim. We're suggesting they provide support and guidance to those entering the jobs (passages), in the following ways:

- Offer regular 360-degree feedback and talks with supervisors. Give people opportunities to ask questions, express concerns, and monitor progress.
- Encourage reflection around new experiences.
- Challenge people to take some risks; push them out of their comfort zones.

- Use coaching to help people talk and receive advice about issues they may not feel comfortable talking to colleagues or bosses about.

To turn open positions into development opportunities, people making the job assignments need to be astute about which positions have the greatest development potential for specific people. Ideally, bosses will know which passages their people haven't been through and put them in positions that allow them to experience diversity and adversity.

Catalyze Professional Passages Through Leadership Development Programs

Organizations should take advantage of programs that prompt them to struggle with significant failures, stretch assignments, new leadership roles, and other passages. We've worked with many companies, including Dell, Johnson & Johnson, Washington Mutual, Novartis, and many others, that have used Action Learning programs to expand their approach to leadership development, combining tough, CEO-driven assignments with "just-in-time information," coaching, assessment, and experiences. These companies and many others have found that these programs work as well as actual on-the-job development. Though Action Learning takes many forms, its essence is providing people with challenging real-world assignments that are packed with adversity and diversity. Action Learning

There ought to be an opportunity when someone is working on a particular problem or issue, that they can come in and say, "Look, I'm not here to get the answer; I'm here to discuss an issue, and I'd like to be able to pick your brain but not feel compelled to do what you tell me. Let's talk through the problem. You've had lots of different experiences; you've been around in the world longer. Let me take the best and leave the rest. Let me just pick your brain." That is a valuable thing in a reporting relationship that rarely gets used.

RAY VIAULT, VICE CHAIRMAN, GENERAL MILLS

assignments are always related to the real business needs and strategies of an organization, and people's performance and growth in these assignments have an impact on their careers. Many times, Action Learning participants select the issues on which their teams will focus—usually hot-button issues for the organization. Participants are encouraged to take risks and try out new ways of thinking and interacting with others; these new behaviors are necessary to handle the assignments effectively. One way or another, the assignments are structured to take people out of their comfort zone. Individuals are asked to work with people or in areas, or even in countries, with which they're not familiar. All the things we've emphasized in navigating the passages—taking time to reflect, learning to look at situations from fresh perspectives, receiving feedback about performance, being aware of weaknesses and learning to manage them—are integral to Action Learning.

Novartis is one company that has taken advantage of Action Learning, using it as the basis for its first-time manager program. These first-time managers pick an issue they're struggling with in their new jobs—often a dilemma of some sort—and they work on these issues in teams. Participants talk about the intensity of the four consecutive days in which they attempt to create strategies to deal with their dilemmas—an intensity similar to what is felt during a passage. More than four thousand Novartis managers have gone through the program, providing the company with a method for developing leaders on a large scale and in a meaningful way.

Benefits of Developing Leadership in a New Way

We've hinted at why companies should acknowledge these passages and integrate them into core people processes, but we'd like to hone in on the specific benefits that companies receive when they do so. The effort does the following:

- *Reduces the risk of great leaders leaving the company.* Every organization has a story of executives who left because they were moved off the fast track (or were never placed on it) and became superstars somewhere else. This happens with surprising frequency. Organizations routinely mislabel good performers as good leaders and average performers as average leaders. This is because they view leadership within a narrow framework. When you look at the whole leader, you realize that a leader is the sum of many parts, both personal and professional. As a result, you begin to see that an individual seems to have become a much better developer of talent after a significant life event or that a volatile, judgmental manager became a much better communicator and motivator after enduring a major lost contract in which customers confronted his actions. No system is foolproof, but a leadership development system that takes a broader view of experience, including passages, will do a much better job of identifying leadership potential.

• *Increases leadership bench strength and diversity.* Most companies can accommodate no more than 15 percent of their employees in leadership development programs. What's more, the ones chosen for these programs are often remarkably homogeneous; they tend to come from similar functions or experiences, share similar attitudes and perspectives about business, and demonstrate an ability to achieve goals, meet deadlines, and do well on performance reviews. In most companies, they even look and dress alike. None of this is necessarily bad, but it prevents a mix of diverse perspectives crucial to innovation, adaptiveness, flexibility, and success. A focus on passages allows organizations to recognize and acknowledge experiences and learnings that may make a great leader but that don't necessarily fall within traditional assessment boundaries. By considering the whole leader when making hiring, promotion, and development decisions, companies won't place artificial limits on who receives leadership positions. Just as important, they will give more development opportunities to a larger number of people, because now such opportunities won't be confined to a short list of high-potentials. Finally, it makes people accountable for their own development. The sole responsibility for development is shifted from the company's shoulder to the individual's, making it a more accessible process.

• *Prevents organizations from firing leaders at times of maximum learning.* This phenomenon rapidly depletes an organization's talent pool. Maximum learning takes place during the passages, especially when executives join companies at senior levels, when they return from an overseas assignment, and when they experience significant failure. Unfortunately, these are also the times when companies terminate executives. People return changed from these experiences. They question policies they always accepted or are more willing to take risks or are more contemplative and willing to listen. When behaviors and attitudes change, it can make senior people uncomfortable. Conformity is still important within organizations, and going through a passage encourages people to be authentic rather than play a role. These returning executives sometimes look like a bad fit for the organization, though in reality they fit perfectly; it's just that they have grown as people and as leaders, and so they appear to be different.

We are often called in to coach senior executives who have been hired at senior levels from other high-performing companies such as GE. These executives have usually been recruited because of their unique experiences, personality, or cultural background, but as they begin to manifest the very qualities for which they have been recruited, the hiring company begins to experience buyer's remorse. Rather than challenge the culture of conformity that is rejecting the transplant, the solution is often to coach the new hire into fitting in and adapting, accepting the leadership style that he or she was recruited to modify. Of course, this process is entirely unconscious, but it does implicate the culture of conformity that characterizes most senior executive ranks.

With the passages in mind, companies will recognize leadership growth for what it is. Not only will this help them avoid removing people who have just made a major step forward as leaders but it will save the company a great deal of money in recruiting and training costs to replace those they have let go.

• *Identifies and defuses ticking time bombs.* In many companies today, a few dysfunctional and even emotionally abusive executives rise to senior levels. All of us are vulnerable to our derailment potential, but at senior levels, executives don't always receive good feedback about how to manage their derailers effectively. Mischievous CEOs who are mostly creative and innovative challenge accepted accounting practices. Arrogant leaders refuse to acknowledge the viewpoint of others. Perfectionists drill down into endless details. Senior executives use fear as a management technique or attempt to cover up their own sense of vulnerability. How are these people promoted into positions of great responsibility? Why don't companies do a better job of identifying those who thwart or de-motivate others, or act without adequate consideration of consequences?

One explanation is that the leadership development and promotion process in most companies today is linear. The better you perform against easily measured outcomes such as financial targets, market share, product development schedules, Six Sigma indices, and the like, the likelier you are to be promoted. Performance assessment usually takes a few factors into consideration when evaluating leadership talent. For senior leaders, however, financial performance should be just one factor among many. Because it is not, companies often overlook the fact that their leaders are performing but not learning. Without reflection, especially from negative events, learning doesn't happen. Obvious dysfunctional behavior can sometimes indicate the need for learning to occur.

The passage model offers companies a way to spot behaviors and attitudes that need to be changed or curtailed and leads to the questions: What is going on, What has gone on, and What needs to happen to encourage this executive to learn and grow?

The real umbrella benefit of these passages to organizations is that it humanizes the system. Consciously or not, companies have modeled their hiring, assessment, and development processes on a financial-planning model. In many companies today, leaders are viewed as assets or liabilities; formulas are used to calculate value. Executives are penalized for significant failures, often spending time in the "penalty box" until their image has been rehabilitated or they are removed. Others are perceived as "not quite on the team" because they arrived through acquisition, worked in the wrong division, don't have a strong advocate within the trusted relationship network of the company, or some aspect in their background is suspect. At the same time, because there is no good way to measure it, executives receive little credit for their ability to develop others, to adapt, or to see an issue from multiple perspectives; neither is credit given for their skill at bringing a diverse group of people together to work with drive and purpose or for their willingness to test nontraditional solutions.

A broader understanding of leadership effectiveness will lead to more intelligent choices in how we recruit, measure, and develop people to become leaders of others. It will be less driven by dry competency models and more focused on a holistic view of how leaders develop and learn, especially through personal and professional passages.

17

An Eight-Step Survive-and-Thrive Guide

If your organization has implemented some of our suggestions from the previous chapter, you will probably find the passages easier to navigate. They may be part of your own leadership development philosophy already. But no matter how your company defines or implements leadership development or recognizes the importance of personal and professional challenges, you must continually learn and grow as a leader. Ultimately, you are responsible for your own development.

Throughout this book, we've suggested ways to view leadership development in a different light and show how you can maximize learning and growth in each of the passages we describe. We've tailored our advice to the nature of each passage, in most cases based on a simple model of reflecting on and redefining the event. You can enlist the help of an executive coach to help you, or you can use this book to do the same thing on your own. Obviously, how you deal with a significant life passage will be very different from how you handle a new project assignment; divorce or the loss of a loved one cannot be equated with a new business responsibility. But all the passages involve growth and development; all contribute to your view of yourself and, ultimately, to your leadership effectiveness.

Not so obviously, perhaps, certain traits and habits help leaders maximize the insights and benefits of all the passages. Based on our interviews, as well as our coaching experiences, we have identified eight distinct "steps" that facilitate the movement through all personal and professional passages. Following the steps will help you avoid the career and personal derailments that lurk within each passage and instead take advantage of the leadership learning in each.

Step 1: Learn Resilience

As the old Timex slogan goes, "It takes a licking and keeps on ticking." Virtually every leader we interviewed showed remarkable resiliency in the face of adversity, especially early in their careers. Many were terminated because they had made stupid mistakes, or they were assigned significant authority for leading a project and missed key deliverables. Sometimes people quit, products didn't work, or the budget was overrun. In some cases, fate intervened, their personal lives unraveled, their company went out of business, or some other out-of-their-control factor took over.

Yet they came back. More than that, they managed to come back as stronger, wiser leaders. For Steve Jobs (CEO of Apple Computer and CEO of Pixar), Sumner Redstone (chairman and CEO of Viacom), and Millard (Mickey) Drexler (chairman and CEO of J. Crew, Inc.), their stories of resilience are legendary. Was this resiliency inherent, or was it nurtured through constant competition? It is difficult to say, though a number of executives related stories from their childhood that suggested the latter. One executive crashed the family car as a teenager and had to call his father for help. When his father arrived, they discovered that the car, though seriously damaged, was still drivable. His father tossed his son the keys and said, "Try to get it home without wrecking it completely."

Whether resilience is the result of nature or nurture, or both, displaying it facilitates the journey through each passage. Relentless optimism and self-confidence are beneficial, especially when events during this passage do not justify these feelings. Without resilience, it is easy to lapse into paralyzing self-doubt, and that is

---

I think resiliency is really important. I have this thing that I use in our leadership course: "Are you a thermometer or are you a thermostat?" A thermometer reflects the temperature around the person, and a thermostat cools when it's too hot and warms when it's too cold. It tries to maintain an even temperature. To the greatest degree, I think, leaders should not be thermometers. They just pass on the temperature that's going on all the time and swing hot and cold and up and down and all of that. Try to be even. It's okay to display some emotion but in my view not to pass the pressure and heat on them all the time.

RAY VIAULT, VICE CHAIRMAN, GENERAL MILLS

---

when events take over. One executive told us that he likes to picture himself as one of those blow-up, life-size balloon-men that children play with. No matter how many times you knock them down, they spring right back up.

Perhaps an image of this balloon-man could find a place in your own consciousness. Remind yourself that if you want to get anywhere in your career or in your life, failure is not permanent or irrevocable, or even the last word on your career. Many of the executives we've worked with have learned to leverage their defeats and disappointments. They have discovered ways to turn their strong negative feelings about an event into positive energy. They can even enjoy the irony of their bad bosses and their own poor choices, resolving to learn and go on.

This doesn't mean they lacked periods of doubt, despair, sadness, or anger. Even today, many years after the event, some of these leaders' voices still betray the strong emotions they felt. But they also were aware of how they felt and articulated their thoughts to others, which cleared the way for them to bounce back. Remember, it is tough to be resilient if you're rigid with anger, fear, or any other strong, unaddressed emotion.

Step 2: Accept Personal Responsibility

In both business and life, our reflex is to blame other people or circumstances for our failures and problems. In business, we say things like this:

> "I wasn't trained properly."

> "We missed last quarter's numbers because of unexpected events."

> "The organization withheld vital resources."

> "Unfortunately, my boss did not support this."

> "A new technology upended our forecasts."

In business, the list goes on endlessly, excuses coming from leaders' mouths with frequency and ease. In personal life, a similar list is at hand: the former spouse wouldn't cooperate, the economy (again) created financial setbacks, the children were ungrateful, and so on. At times, it seems as if we live in a culture of avoiding personal responsibility.

All this may be true, and bad things do happen. But leaders can be divided into two groups: those who take responsibility and those who don't. Learning and growth in a difficult or even positive passage is impossible if you don't take personal responsibility. You need this responsibility to engage in constructive self-examination. Without it, you'll turn your attention outward, ignoring how a particular event affects you or what your role in bringing it about might have been.

To help leaders accept responsibility, we frequently use the SARA model (see Chapter One) for receiving feedback or dealing with negative events. Understanding these predictable reactions makes it possible to increase self-awareness:

S — Shock
A — Anger
R — Rejection
A — Acceptance

One of the executives we interviewed had been passed over for a promotion he felt he richly deserved. He made a conscious effort to manage his response by working through the four letters of the model. Of course, he didn't need the model to react first with shock and then with anger to the company's decision. But the third word, *rejection*, was useful; it made him aware that he was rejecting the possibility that he was culpable. Thinking about this issue and talking about it with a coach helped him realize that his arrogance may have been a legitimate reason why the company felt he wasn't ready to take on this new leadership role. Over time, he came to accept that he himself was responsible for being passed over. The acceptance motivated him to work at moderating his arrogance. And as his arrogance moderated, he began receiving more important assignments from his boss, and this gave him hope that he might receive the promotion he desired at some point in the future.

Step 3: Reflect

We know we've emphasized this step in many of the passages, but it is the basis for leadership learning and the way to avoid repeating an experience. If you don't understand why you are succeeding, you're operating at the level of an efficient machine, not an effective leader. If you don't understand why you failed, you are vulnerable to the recurrence of the same events.

Reflection facilitates understanding. Almost all the leaders we interviewed talked about the importance of reflection, though they didn't always use this term. One executive, a former military officer, for instance, referred to "After Action Review"—a process by which commanders analyze what went right and wrong after a military engagement. He routinely did the same thing in the business world. If you recall David Kolb's learning theory, presented in Chapter Two, you'll understand how reflection is absolutely essential to learning. Although some of us are more inclined to reflect than others, everyone can make it a conscious part of their response to each passage.

During Action Learning programs, executives participate together in addressing a current business or strategy challenge for the corporation. What differentiates Action Learning from working on a task team is the process of reflecting and then engaging in self- and team challenge. This accelerates learning, encourages self-insight, and creates the conditions for leadership growth. But you don't need to participate in an Action Learning program to reap the same benefits. Make reflection part of your everyday repertoire, rigorously challenge old assumptions, review the action once it's over, and you'll make yourself a better leader.

After an event triggers a passage in your life, ask yourself the same questions an executive coach might ask you:

Why did this happen to me (or to someone I care about)?

Did my actions or attitudes contribute in some way to the event?

If I had acted differently, might the event have turned out differently?

Do I feel angry, sad, or guilty about what took place? Why?

If I could turn back the clock and change something I said or did, what would it be?

These and similar types of questions will give you the material to reflect on in every passage (see Figure 17.1 for more ideas).

Step 4: Seek Support from Your Partner, Family, Friends, and Professionals

Passages of both diversity and adversity create stress. When you are pushing your performance limits or dealing with failure and loss, you can feel isolated. Many leaders remarked that when they were struggling during a passage, it seemed like the event was happening

Figure 17.1. Three Steps to Enhancing Leadership Effectiveness
Through Reflection.

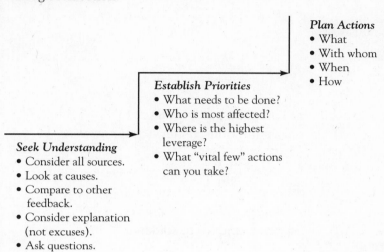

Plan Actions
- What
- With whom
- When
- How

Establish Priorities
- What needs to be done?
- Who is most affected?
- Where is the highest leverage?
- What "vital few" actions can you take?

Seek Understanding
- Consider all sources.
- Look at causes.
- Compare to other feedback.
- Consider explanation (not excuses).
- Ask questions.

only to them. Though it obviously happens to everyone, it doesn't feel that way. A sense of loneliness and isolation is not only typical, it intensifies at the top of the hierarchy where, by definition, there are even fewer organizational peers.

Giving in to a sense of isolation makes it easy to lapse into defeatism. Negative mind-sets inhibit change. We are surprised by how many leaders engage executive coaches for support but will not engage family and friends for support during difficult times. Many leaders still equate excessive confidence with competence and adopt an "I'm in control" pose, not even confiding in those to whom they are emotionally close. Some leaders, especially men, simply aren't accustomed to expressing their feelings about work and career and may not like admitting to others that they feel vulnerable (see Figure 17.2). A recent study of CEOs found that their greatest fear was that others might glimpse their own felt sense of vulnerability.

Figure 17.2. Work-Life Experiences.

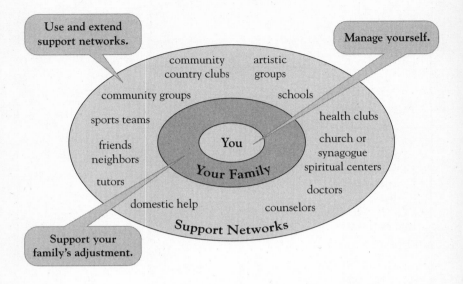

The increasing popularity of executive coaching demonstrates the importance of support, especially professional insights. It also highlights the sense of isolation many executives experience today. In many of the executive leadership programs that CDR International conducts for global companies, we provide a one-on-one coaching experience for participants over the course of a week. For many executives, this contact with an objective listener and helper is the highlight of the week, because it enables them to open up about their leadership issues with an expert—to unburden, reflect, and converse. The experience accelerates their learning and admits them to the possibility of gaining support for issues they felt they must address alone.

Most of our interviewees expressed the following sentiment: "I would have never made it if it had not been for the support of ___." Emotional support helps you rebound, to recognize that you are not alone in your struggle or failure. This helps make the passage tolerable and keeps you listening, questioning, and remaining open-minded.

Step 5: Develop and Use a Professional Network

Passages often mean change, and change may impel you to find a new assignment within your company, to seek greater responsibility, even to leave the company, change direction, or search for something else. These passages also drive people to seek out others for information about opportunities, advice, political insights about the company, or late-breaking developments. It makes sense to establish internal and external networks of people you can rely on for these purposes. Ideally, you will have established these networks prior to entering the passage (it takes time to build networks), and you may lack that time or focus during a passage.

> To me, that's what life is about—pilgrims on a journey. We go through life together and if we can help each other, that's a good thing. I don't like the word mentor. I like to think of it as a friendship. It's a two-way street, and we learn from each other.
>
> BILL GEORGE, FORMER CHAIRMAN AND CEO, MEDTRONIC

Plugging into a network means making a conscious effort to talk to and meet with others about the issues raised by a given passage. As we've emphasized, exposing your vulnerabilities—especially using the phrase, "I don't know"—creates learning for yourself and, as a leader, you create learning for others. Opening up to others can facilitate change. Someone in your network may suggest a coach who can help you address a performance issue or may give you a lead for a job that offers the responsibility and challenging projects you need. This network may also affect your personal life, linking you to other ways of developing and growing as a leader, including volunteer assignments, participation in religious activities, support groups, or new friends. Leaders are as smart, capable, and wise as the networks they can call on when they need it.

Step 6: Seek Refuge

For some people, this step means going to a place, such as a house in the country, a favorite retreat, or even a room within one's home. For others, it means activity—everything from sports, to art, to other forms of release. For still others, it means meditation, yoga, prayer, or down time. Though these retreats vary, they all provide a place for people to escape and re-energize. A number of the leaders we interviewed noted that these places or activities allowed them to separate themselves from the turmoil in their jobs or their lives. It was liberating for them not to have to think about work or a difficult aspect of their personal life for a few hours or days, and it was critical for them to develop the sense of distance and detachment that leads to greater objectivity.

The passages are intense, and leaders can only endure so much intensity before it becomes counterproductive. In order to lead, you need to manage your energy, and thus you need a temporary escape. When you return, you will have more energy to focus on the issues that the passages brought to the surface and greater insight into the demands placed on you and what needs to be done; you will be less likely to escape in counterproductive ways such as denial or addictions, or in blaming others.

Step 7: Gain Perspective

"What I learned about myself," one executive told us when talking about a particular passage in his life, "was worth all the pain." Rising above a passage and seeing it from a higher perspective helps put difficult events in context. Even great leaders become so immersed in the pace of life, the demands of others, and the details of working in complex, interdependent organizations that it is possible to miss the larger meaning of events. We can't see that a temporary setback at work, such as losing a key customer, missing a projection, being passed over, reporting to a disliked peer, or some other event that completely absorbs us loses its significance when a more significant event such as loss, grief, or illness arrives. But leaders regularly tell us that even those events, as painful and difficult as they can be, constitute the flow of life and ultimately contribute to a greater sense of meaning when enough objectivity and detachment can be invoked. In the heat of the moment, we forget these truths. This is why it's so difficult to learn from our experiences while they are occurring. We become mired in our fears, anxiety, or negative feelings, or we replay our mistakes ad infinitum. We are unable to view our feelings, our situation, or ourselves with any degree of objectivity.

The literal nature of this step is that you move away from your situation, gain some distance on it. The new viewing angle provides a degree of objectivity that lets you see your passage within a larger context. One female marketing executive we have worked with, for instance, was struggling with the need to report to a particularly bad supervisor. What helped her get through it and learn from it was perspective. As she said, "I used to confuse my role as vice president of marketing with my identity. Now I know that I don't own my job, and it doesn't own me." It is common for people to confuse their identities with their jobs. In non-passage times, it is hard to achieve this perspective. Leaders in roles with significant responsibility and authority especially are tempted to blur their role with their sense of self. They become caught up in peoples constantly needing them, asking their opinions, and valuing what they have to say.

A passage is an opportunity to see a job—or any event in life— from a broader perspective. A career roadblock or uncomfortable circumstance shakes your confidence, your routine, and your sense of control. Suddenly, you have a chance to see things clearly. Force yourself to take advantage of this fresh view, and remind yourself that you are participating in a leadership development experience. It will make negative events in a passage more palatable and understandable. It will also provide you with insight about what is important in your career and your life. The female marketing executive resolved to not let her role dominate her and to develop a clear understanding of her priorities, including making more time for others. As she put it, "I will no longer do things that I don't want to do." It was a statement she could never have made until she went through the passage.

Step 8: Take Risks

Essentially, what it means to take risks is that you must embrace the passages rather than escape them. From the passages perspective, taking risks as a leader requires purposefully inviting adversity and diversity into your life. Some people attempt to control their careers to minimize risk: turning down uncomfortable assignments, not moving their families because of the upheaval it creates, refusing to challenge the conventional wisdom of their team or organization, or not engaging their boss with any authentic feedback. This play-it-safe behavior helps people avoid the new experiences and adverse circumstances that come with each passage, thus curtailing their development.

In Action Learning leadership development programs, we intentionally force executives to move outside their comfort zone by engaging in such diverse experiences as climbing mountains, interviewing citizens in a developing country, meeting government leaders, or volunteering in a homeless shelter. An athlete improves performance by pushing his personal performance edge, and the analogy holds true for leaders. You cannot expect to evolve as a leader without placing yourself in unfamiliar situations or experiencing pain. Risks provide you with both. This doesn't mean engaging in needlessly hazardous behaviors such as confronting others with no reason or data, or signing up for outcomes or projects for which success is not only difficult but probably impossible. But it does mean making a habit of exposing yourself to situations where you feel uncomfortable and confronting your feelings and flaws. In our experience, the good leaders have taken personal risks repeatedly throughout their careers, especially in their passages, and they work to minimize the creeping conservatism that sometimes accompanies success.

The Last Step: Retirement

Incorporating these eight steps into your leadership outlook will prepare you for the last passage of a career: retirement. What constitutes retirement is rapidly changing, but at some point each of us will come to the end of full-time professional involvement and engage in something else. Each time you go through a passage in a conscious, reflective manner, you gain a measure of self-knowledge and maturity. It helps you to know yourself and to understand your values and priorities. As a result, retirement doesn't become an end point but a passage of its own in the best sense of the word. You are aware of what you value and how to translate it into life after full-time work. Whether you decide to use your skills and knowledge in a volunteer role or travel, or even in a new part-time job, you will make this decision, fully aware of what you want to get out of the remaining years of your life. This is quite different from people who enter retirement with little awareness of their values and beliefs, of what makes life meaningful for them.

We coach many senior executives who have invested their entire life, to that point, in their professional role. They have not developed interests, hobbies, or even strong relationships with significant others because of the demands of their role and the time and commitment they have given to it. They have never separated their identity from their work role, and for them, retirement rebounds them into their early twenties: they must struggle, once again, to determine what interests them, what they want, what they want to pursue, and how they want to spend time. This is a rebuilding challenge that can be avoided by paying attention long before retirement to how you want to spend your time and your life, in addition to your leadership role.

Passing on Your Experiences

We would like to leave you with one additional suggestion about how you can use these passages. We have noted that emotional intelligence is forged in the passages and have described how struggles and new experiences help you become more empathic, a better communicator, and a more trusted and trusting leader. As a result, you become better able to help others navigate these passages successfully, simultaneously fulfilling another leadership requirement. You become sensitive to what others are going through and the support they require. If a direct report returns from maternity leave, your unconscious attitude won't be, "Let's see if she can keep up." Instead, your approach as a leader will become, "What can I do to help?" A primary responsibility of a leader is to grow other people; as a passage-tested executive, you are in an ideal position to fulfill this responsibility.

The thirteen predictable, intense passages can certainly be stressful, confusing, and emotionally volatile periods in your life. They are also the foundation with which you can become a stronger, more humane, and more effective leader. With insight, reflection, and a strong dose of self-forgiveness, you can turn the experiences of your life and career into personal growth for yourself and for others.

Bibliography

Badaracco, J. L., Jr. *Defining Moments: Choosing Between Right and Right.* Boston: Harvard Business School Press, 1997.

Badaracco, J. L., Jr. *Leading Quietly: An Unorthodox Guide to Doing the Right Thing.* Boston: Harvard Business School Press, 2002.

Badaracco, J. L., Jr., and Ellsworth, R. R. *Leadership and the Quest for Integrity.* Boston: Harvard Business School Press, 1993.

Bennis, W. G., Spreitzer, G. M., and Cummings, T. (eds.). *The Future of Leadership: Today's Top Leadership Thinkers Speak to Tomorrow's Leaders.* New York: Wiley, 2001.

Block, P. *Stewardship: Choosing Service Over Self-Interest.* San Francisco: Berrett-Koehler, 1996.

Bridges, W. *Transitions: Strategies for Coping with the Difficult, Painful, and Confusing Times in Your Life.* Cambridge: Perseus, 1980.

Bronson, P. O. *What Should I Do with My Life?* New York: Random House, 2002.

Cashman, K. *Awakening the Leader Within.* New York: Wiley, 2003.

Charan, R., Drotter, S., and Noel, J. *The Leadership Pipeline.* San Francisco: Jossey-Bass 2001.

Ciampa, D., and Watkins, M. *Right from the Start.* Boston: Harvard Business School Press, 1999.

Citrin, J. M., and Smith, R. A. *The 5 Patterns of Extraordinary Careers.* New York: Crown Business, 2003.

Collins, J. *Good to Great: Why Some Companies Make the Leap . . . and Others Don't.* New York: HarperCollins, 2001.

Conger, J. A. *Spirit at Work: Discovering the Spirituality in Leadership*. San Francisco: Jossey-Bass, 1994.

Dotlich, D. L., and Cairo, P. C. *Action Coaching: How to Leverage Individual Performance for Company Success*. San Francisco: Jossey-Bass, 2001.

Dotlich, D. L., and Cairo, P. C. *Unnatural Leadership: Ten New Leadership Instincts*. San Francisco: Jossey-Bass, 2002.

Dotlich, D. L., and Noel, J. L. *Action Learning: How the World's Top Companies Are Re-Creating Their Leaders and Themselves*. San Francisco: Jossey-Bass, 1998.

Egan, G. *Working the Shadow Side: A Guide to Positive Behind-the-Scenes Management*. San Francisco: Jossey-Bass, 1994.

Goleman, D. *Emotional Intelligence*. New York: Bantam Books, 1997.

Goleman, D. *Working with Emotional Intelligence*. New York: Bantam Books, 1998.

Graves, S., and Addington, T. *Life and Work on Leadership*. San Francisco: Jossey-Bass, 2002.

Handy, C. *The Hungry Spirit: Beyond Capitalism: A Quest for Purpose in the Modern World*. New York: Broadway Books, 1999.

Handy, C. *Waiting for the Mountain to Move: Reflections on Work and Life*. San Francisco: Jossey-Bass, 1999.

Heifetz, R. *Leading Without Easy Answers*. Cambridge, Mass.: Belknap Press, 1994.

Heifetz, R., and Linsky, M. *Leadership on the Line: Staying Alive Through the Dangers of Leading*. Boston: Harvard Business School Press, 2002.

Holden, R., and Renshaw, B. *Balancing Work and Life*. London: Dorling Kindersley, 2002.

Horney, K. *Neurosis and Human Growth*. New York: Norton, 1950.

Jampolsky, G. G., and Cirincione, D. V. *Change Your Mind, Change Your Life: Concepts in Attitudinal Healing*. New York: Bantam Books, 1994.

Katzenbach, J. R. *Teams at the Top*. Boston: Harvard Business School Press, 1998.

Keeny, B. *Everyday Soul: Awakening the Spirit in Daily Life*. Riverhead Books, 1997.

Kleiner, A. *Who Really Matters*. New York: Doubleday, 2003.

Koestenbaum, P. *The Heart of Business*. Saybrook Publishing, 1991.

Kolb, D. A. *Experiential Learning*. Englewood Cliffs: Prentice Hall, 1984.

Kunde, J. *Corporate Religion: Building a Strong Company Through Personality and Corporate Soul.* New York: Financial Times/Prentice Hall, 2000.

Levine, R., Locke, C., Searls, D., and Weinberger, D. *The Cluetrain Manifesto: The End of Business As Usual.* Colorado: Perseus Press, 2000.

Loehr, J., and Schwartz, T. *The Power of Full Engagement.* New York: Free Press, 2003.

Lundin, W., and Lundin, K. *The Healing Manager: How to Build Quality Relationships and Productive Cultures at Work.* San Francisco: Berrett-Koehler, 1993.

Marrs, D. *Executive in Passage: Career in Crisis—the Door to Uncommon Fulfillment.* Los Angeles: Barrington Sky, 1990.

Marshall, E. M. *Building Trust at the Speed of Change.* New York: AMACOM, 2000.

McCall, M. W., Jr., and Lombardo, M. M. "Off the Track: Why and How Successful Executives Get Derailed" (Tech. Rep. no. 21). Greensboro, N.C.: Center for Creative Leadership, 1983.

McCall, M. W., Jr., Lombardo, M. M., and Morrison, A. M. *Lessons of Experience.* Lexington, Mass.: Lexington Press, 1988.

Ogilvy, J. *Living Without a Goal: Finding the Freedom to Live a Creative Innovative and Fulfilled Life.* New York: Currency/Doubleday, 1995.

O'Neill, J. R. *The Paradox of Success: When Winning at Work Means Losing at Life—A Book of Renewal for Leaders.* New York: Traches, 1994.

Pearce, T. *Leading Out Loud.* San Francisco: Jossey-Bass, 1995.

Pearson, C., and Seivert, S. *Magic at Work: Camelot, Creative Leadership, and Everyday Miracles.* New York: Doubleday, 1995.

Quinn, R. E. *Deep Change: Discovering the Leader Within.* San Francisco: Jossey-Bass, 1996.

Schwartz, T. *What Really Matters: Searching for Wisdom in America.* New York: Bantam Books, 1996.

Scott, S. *Fierce Conversations.* New York: Viking, 2002.

Shaw, R. B. *Trust in the Balance: Building Successful Organizations on Results, Integrity, and Concern.* San Francisco: Jossey-Bass, 1997.

Stoltz, P. G. *Adversity Quotient and Work.* New York: HarperCollins, 2000.

Sussman, L., Deep, S., and Stiber, A. *Lost and Found.* New York: Crown Business, 2004.

Thompson, M. C. *The Congruent Life: Following the Inward Path to Fulfilling Work and Inspired Leadership.* San Francisco: Jossey-Bass, 2000.

Warner, J. *Aspirations of Greatness*. New York: Wiley, 2002.

Weisinger, H. *Emotional Intelligence at Work*. San Francisco: Jossey-Bass, 1998.

Whyte, D. *The Heart Aroused: Poetry and the Preservation of the Soul in Corporate America*. New York: Currency/Doubleday, 1996.

About the Authors

David L. Dotlich is the CEO and managing partner of CDR International, a Mercer Delta Company (www.mercerdelta.com), and partner of Mercer Delta Consulting—a global consulting firm that helps companies define and implement strategies to enhance leadership effectiveness and manage change. He is a business adviser to CEOs and senior executives of global corporations such as Johnson & Johnson, Bank of America, Intel, Washington Mutual, UBS, Nike, and many others. He is the author of five best-selling leadership books: *Action Coaching: Why CEOs Fail; Action Learning: How the World's Best Companies Develop Their Leaders and Themselves,* and the breakthrough book, *Unnatural Leadership: Going Against Intuition and Instinct to Develop Ten New Leadership Instincts* (all published by Jossey-Bass). Previously, he was executive vice president with Honeywell International and Groupe Bull. He can be contacted at david.dotlich@mercerdelta.com.

James L. Noel has over twenty years' experience in developing senior leaders and executive coaching. His perspective on leadership development was shaped by his tenure at Crotonville—General Electric's leadership development institute—where he was manager of executive education and leadership effectiveness. Previously, he was vice president for executive development, Citibank; earlier, he was assistant dean of the College of General Studies, The

George Washington University. He is a principal with CDR International and Mercer Delta Consulting and is the coauthor of two books: *The Leadership Pipeline* and *Action Learning: How the World's Best Companies Develop Their Leaders and Themselves*.

Norman Walker was, until recently, head of human resources for Novartis; he was a member of the executive committee reporting to the chairman and CEO. In this role, he established business-driven human resource processes to the line and was instrumental in the creation of leading-edge talent and executive development programs. Previously, he was head of human resources for Kraft Europe and Jacobs Suchard; before that, he held senior executive European human resource positions with Grand Met and Ford Motor Company. He consults with senior executives and CEOs on people and leadership development issues; he can be contacted at n.walker@normanwalker.ch.

Index

A

Acceptance: in acquistion-or-merger passage, 122; as emotional reaction to negative events, 26–27, 205; in letting-go-of-ambition passage, 162–163; in personal upheaval passage, 174

Accidents, 30–32

Accountability, personal, 11; accepting, 204–205; in general manager position, 73; learning from failure and, 26. *See also* Responsibility

Accounting practices, creative, 199

Achievement: basic need for, 34–35, 162; focus on, in losing-faith-in-the-system passage, 185; redefining and measuring, 164

Acquisition-or-merger passage, 119–131; assessment for fit in, 128; case example of, 126–128; challenges of, 120–122; with competitor company, 120, 121; cultural adaptation in, 120–121; emotional responses to, 122, 129; growing in, 122–131; for leaders of acquiring company, 131; opportunities in, 130–131; practical steps for handling, 128–131; psychological impact of, 119, 120–122, 130

Action, taking: after being fired or passed over, 115–116; about bad boss, 104

Action Learning: cultural immersion experiences in, 133, 142; experiential learning and, 23; for first-time managers, 51, 196; for leadership develop-ment, 195–196; reflection in, 206; risk taking in, 212–213; in stretch assignments, 68–69

Action Learning: How the World's Top Companies Develop Their Leaders and Themselves (Dotlich and Noel), 69

Adaptation: creating a new identity and, 27–30; to new company culture, 36–39, 120–121

Adaptive change, learning attitudes and, 23–26

Adventurer's mind-set, 139

Adversity: career and work, 9, 17; learn-ing from, 14–17, 30–32, 193–194; life, 17; psychological strength from, 43–44. *See also* Learning, from pas-sages

Affiliation: basic need for, 34–35, 162; transition of, in joining-a-company passage, 38–39

After Action Review, 206

Airline industry, 160–161

Ambiguity, hang-in-there mentality and, 77–78

Ambition: achievement *versus*, 164; defining success and, 157–159; letting go of, as passage, 157–166. *See also* Letting-go-of-ambition passage

Andersen Worldwide, 124, 125

Anger: about acquisition or merger, 122, 129; at being fired or passed over, 107, 108–109, 113–114, 117; as emotional reaction to negative events, 26–27, 205